About Time!

120 tips for those
with no time

Robyn Pearce

REED

ALSO BY THE AUTHOR:

Getting a Grip on Time

ROBYN PEARCE'S WEBSITE ADDRESS IS

http://www.gettingagripontime.com

Reed Publishing
Te Karuhi tā tāpui o Reed (Aotearoa) (NZ) Ltd

Established in 1907, Reed is New Zealand's largest
book publisher, with over 300 titles in print.

For details on all these books visit our website:
www.reed.co.nz

Published by Reed Books, a division of Reed Publishing (NZ) Ltd,
39 Rawene Rd, Birkenhead, Auckland.
Associated companies, branches and representatives
throughout the world.

ISBN 0 7900 0787 8
First pubplished 2001
Reprinted 2003, 2004

Printed in New Zealand

To my dear husband, Mike. Thanks for your uncomplaining help in running the house as this book churned out from under my flying fingers.

To the many subscribers and contributors to our 'Top Time Tips' e-zine, delivered electronically each month. Your input has been greatly appreciated.

To the thousands of participants and attendees at speeches and workshops around seven countries – this book would never have been born without you. I learn from every group I work with. Thank you for your willingness to share.

About the Author

Robyn Pearce has learnt her knowledge and skills about time management and productivity from the ground up. In fact, she's made just about all the mistakes you could imagine! What's more, she's survived! From humble beginnings as a farmer's wife, mother of six (including an intellectually handicapped foster son), then a solo mother and real estate agent, Robyn *had* to learn better time management skills — or sink! For years no one else in the house would answer the phone. She's been kicked out of meetings because she was late. She's burnt out numerous times from overwork. In fact, she thinks she wrote the handbook on stress! Finally a friend pointed her in the direction of a decent diary and a few key time management principles. Since then she's turned her biggest weakness into a major strength. As a keynote speaker, trainer and author, since 1992, Robyn has been sharing her experiences and knowledge with thousands of clients around the Asia-Pacific region, helping them win their time battles. She is the New Zealand Director of TimeLogic, the Time Management company she has founded, which has offices in Australia and New Zealand. Her first book, *Getting a Grip on Time*, has remained in print since it was first published in 1996. She writes for many publications and regularly appears on television and radio.

At the website of the TimeLogic Corporation, you'll find all manner of further resources to assist you on your time-learning journey, including a number mentioned in this book.

www.gettingagripontime.com

Contents

Introduction

Hi there, you with this book in your hands. Perhaps someone's given it to you, and you're wondering what the hidden agenda is. Maybe you're browsing and something's tickled your fancy. Or you're desperate, and you hope this will be the panacea you seek.

You might have read some typical time management books before, and you're thinking, 'What's different about this one?' Maybe you know all the basic principles – you just wish a genie would wave a magic wand. The ideas are fine, but that damned 'discipline' word gets in the way! Perhaps you get brassed off by all these 'perfect' writers. Don't they ever slip up, have a messy office, procrastinate, or run late for important meetings? Secretly you're sure no one can be that perfect, and if they are, you're sure they must be both boring and completely lacking in understanding of what it's like to live in your shoes.

Well, let's come clean right up front. I'm certainly not perfect, but it is fun practising. In fact, my serious challenges with time are what drove me to learn more about it. The good news is that it is possible to improve if you're 'time challenged'.

These days everyone seems challenged about something – vertically challenged, horizontally challenged, weight challenged (is everyone in the whole world too fat or too thin!?), spatially challenged, attention-span challenged and so on. So, let's coin a new one – 'time-choices challenged'. In other words, you drive yourself and everyone around you nuts in your search for more time, more space, less paper and less stress. You wish you had more time to enjoy life, less time at the office, and that you could make enough money to live in the exotic destination of your choice.

Using our time well has two major elements to it: one, knowing how to plan and prioritise and make wise choices with our wonderful and precious gift of life, and two, learning the shortcuts that save us time minute by minute and day by day.

My first book, *Getting a Grip on Time*, deals thoroughly with planning and prioritising, and then investigates many of the regular time issues people have, including phones, delegation, meetings, procrastination and paper-handling.

This book has a very different purpose: to share with you a selection of quick, snappy and useful time-savers. They've been gleaned from a variety of sources over a period of four years and include contributions from subscribers to our monthly 'Top Time Tips' e-zine. Dip into it in spare minutes; use the index to guide you to your specific challenges. You'll find items for the corporate office, the home-based office, and even some for your personal life.

Robyn Pearce
August 2001

*P*rioritising
and
planning

Key points

1 Effective prioritising is the major time challenge for most people, yet it is so simple.

2 Procrastination is not the key problem with time management — it's lack of clarity about what's important.

3 Once you learn to develop a proactive focus in all areas of your life, including the small things, you conquer the big things. The results will amaze you.

4 Weekly planning is the fastest way to obtain focus on important tasks and achieve great results.

5 You keep appointments with other people, don't you? How about making appointments with yourself for the things that really matter?

6 If every day you achieve the top few items on your 'To Do' list, in a very short number of years you will achieve success beyond your wildest dreams.

7 If possible, use only one diary, planner or organiser.

8 Choose a diary system you enjoy using.

9 Owl or fowl? Plan your day when you're sharp.

10 'No' is one of your most powerful time management tools.

 Effective prioritising is the major time challenge for most people, yet it is so simple. The hard part is disciplining yourself to stay with the current 'main thing'.

Prioritising consists of five elements:

➡ Know the big picture. If you don't know what really matters to you in life (goals, mission, purpose, call it what you will) you might be very busy majoring in minor things. Some people, without thought, make minor things their lifetime's work.

➡ Understand the difference between urgent and important. As General Eisenhower said during World War II, the things that are really important are rarely urgent, and a surprising number of urgent matters are not really important.

➡ Develop a proactive focus so that every day you spend some time working on something long-term important but not urgent – anything that will make a long-term difference in your life. It might only be five minutes' worth of activity, or it could be a part of a major project.

➡ Plan your activities for the week, including scheduling in appointments with yourself for things that matter but would commonly be left until you 'have time'!

➡ Every morning, at the beginning of the day, do your daily planning.

 Procrastination is not the key problem with time management — it's lack of clarity about what's important.

Have you got a clear idea of everything you want to achieve in the next twelve months? If so, is it written down? I ask this question of most of the groups I work with, and typically about 5 percent of the room will have written goals. (Maybe that's why they're with me!)

Think of it this way. Picture a very rainy day and a house with blocked guttering. It's a while since anyone cleared out the sticks and twigs in the spouting and so the guttering doesn't cope with the deluge. Water is everywhere – spilling over the gutters, flooding the paths and gardens. However, if someone were to clear the blockage in the guttering, the water would drain away very quickly.

I see our brains working the same way. So often our minds feel overwhelmed with too many choices. It's as if we're punching cotton wool. Result – overload, confusion, lack of focus, no clarity, and indecision. Our mental drains are blocked. The fastest way to unblock them is to pick up a writing stick (otherwise known as a pen or your fast-flashing keyboard fingers) and jot down everything currently rattling around in that necktop computer of yours. As soon as things are down on paper (or the electronic equivalent) the flood of ideas is channelled and easy to manage. There is an immediate reduction of pressure (stress) and we're in control.

People are usually reasonable at planning the small things in life. How silly not to do it with the things that matter. Otherwise, we may wake up when we're old, saying to ourselves, 'I wish I'd done ...' Bit late then, mate.

So, what excuse have you got now? Get to it – it'll take you only about 20–30 minutes to write down what you'd like to achieve, in all areas of your life, for the next twelve months. Be spontaneous, go with the top-of-mind ideas, and have fun. Try these headings (they cover everything):

Self and well-being
Spirituality
Business and career
Home and family
Community and humanity

 Once you learn to develop a proactive focus in all areas of your life, including the small things, you conquer the big things. The results will amaze you.

What does 'proactive' really mean, you may ask? I see it as anything, large or small, that isn't urgent — but it is of high importance. Proactive action will make a difference to future events. Many proactive activities take only a few minutes — but there are always other things that can consume those minutes.

So many people say, 'That's not urgent, I'll get round to it — later.' They're always waiting for a reasonable chunk of time, the ideal moment, the gap in the day. Guess what? Ideal moments are very coy and they come but rarely. You have to grasp them by their elusive coat tails, boss them around and take control.

We all have the same amount of time. The major difference between those who just box along and those who have very successful and richly fulfilled lives is that successful folk have learnt to develop a proactive focus. (And money is not the only measure for richness.) On a daily basis, they look for tasks both big and small, that will make a long-term difference in their lives.

Ask yourself these questions every day:

➡ What can I do today that will have a long-term impact on my life?

➡ What can I do today that, when done, will not have to be repeated?

➡ What is the most important task to do today?

 **Weekly planning is the fastest way to obtain focus on important tasks and achieve great results.**

Many people operate with random 'To Do' lists, a melee of ideas doing loop-the-loops in their heads, and lots of good intentions. At the butt end of many a day they find themselves dissatisfied with the outcome.

The way to tie all your goals, your proactive focus and your good intentions together is to block in regular slots of time for the things that matter on some form of weekly planning sheet.

Today, many business people will use the computer systems they have on their desks. Or, you may be the proud owner of a personal digital assistant (PDA), alias a handheld electronic diary such as a Palm, Sharp or Casio. These tools can very readily be used for weekly planning.

Some paper-based systems have a weekly view, but try and find one with the columns running down the page rather than across: it's easier to see the gaps and sight what you've got on for the week. Such systems are hard to come by so I've designed my own weekly planning page.

Check our website (http://www.gettingagripontime.com) and you'll find ordering details. While you're on the website you're welcome to subscribe to our free 'Top Time Tips' e-zine.

You keep appointments with other people, don't you? How about making appointments with yourself for the things that really matter?

Once you've got a weekly planning tool that works for you, each week make appointments with yourself to attend to the proactive important tasks, including time with family and friends, and personal time for yourself.

Sometimes these appointments will still have to be shifted, but the act of shifting an appointment makes most of us take pause. It helps make you more aware of your choices. If you do have to move a personal appointment, make sure you reschedule it.

If you're being too ambitious in what you think you can achieve, the action of having to move things helps you realise the stress you're putting on yourself. Hair shirts went out of fashion when Sir Thomas More was beheaded in the Tower in 1535 – don't turn yourself into a martyr by trying to be all things to all people.

 If every day you achieve the top few items on your 'To Do' list, in a very short number of years you will achieve success beyond your wildest dreams.

Most people know what they should do for the day, but they allow events to overtake them. They dodge frenetically from crisis to crisis, task to task. Instead, try this very simple process.

➡ At the beginning of the day (or the night before), make a list of all the things you want to do for the day, in no particular order.

➡ Identify the top five activities, and number them 1 through 5, wherever they are on the list. Don't bother to number the rest of the list yet, just the top five.

➡ Start at No. 1, and don't leave the job until you've finished it, gone as far as you wish to go, or as far as you're able to go.

➡ When interruptions come, as they always do, ask yourself, 'Is this new activity more important than the one I'm working on?' If it's not, add the new thing to your list, put it out of eye-range so it doesn't distract you, and stay focused on the more important activity. If it is more important, put the other task aside, work on the new job, and when completed go back to your list (which has been considered and thought about before the day started bossing you around!).

➡ Each time you move to the next number, check the list. If something that's jumped on the list during the day is of higher priority than the activity you'd planned to do, give it lead position. The other things won't go away, but because they're on the list, instead of them jostling for mind space you can keep them under tight rein and they won't distract you.

➥ If there's any day left once the top five and their relevant queue jumpers have been handled, go back to the list and number off another five. The reason you don't prioritise your entire list at the beginning of the day is that you would have wasted time — some things you'll never get to.

This simple technique earned management consultant Ivy Lee $25,000 back in the late 1920s–30s when he taught his method to Charles Schwab, head of Bethlehem Steel. Years later, when a newspaper reporter asked Mr Schwab why he paid so much for such seemingly simple advice (Mr Lee had merely asked him to send a cheque for what he thought it was worth once he and his managers had used it for a month), he replied that it was the most important advice he'd ever received, and largely responsible for driving Bethlehem Steel through to the number one position it subsequently enjoyed.

Keep your planning simple.

If possible, use only one diary, planner or organiser.

As soon as you start using more than one planning tool you're setting yourself up for potential disaster. Something is bound to slip through the net, and before you can say Jack Robinson* you'll be dusting yourself down — with a red face. How embarrassing!

Worse than that, even if you're clever enough to check all your diaries every day, the stress you put on yourself is quite unnecessary. There's always a nagging fear that you might forget something.

Don't get hooked up with what your 'planning tool' is called — the name doesn't matter, the process does. Some of the diary companies get quite pedantic about calling their products organisers rather than diaries. Who cares? It's the job that's important, not the semantics.

So you've got a home planner, a company intranet system for some things, and you really like your paper diary as well? Or you have a family diary on the fridge or a wall calendar at home, a small pocket diary for personal things, the big planning is on a whiteboard on the office wall, your goals and work targets are buried in your in-tray, and your day-to-day work stuff is basically a 'To Do' list in a cheap annual diary from the stationery department. I'd be confused too!

---

* Here's something for your next trivial pursuit quiz. Did you know that the saying 'Before you can say Jack Robinson' came from the days when Sir Jack Robinson was the Governor of the Tower of London, and the kings and queens of England had rather permanent ways to dispose of their rivals? If you didn't watch your manners, before the worthy Jack's name could be uttered, you'd find yourself minus a head!

There's no simple answer, but see what you can amalgamate. Make your own diary the key source of everything that's important to you. This is how it becomes a planning tool as well as a diary.

If you use an electronic desk-based system, find out how to make personal matters private (almost all systems allow you to do this). Then run off a paper copy and carry it with you whenever you're away from your desk (including home time). As soon as you return to your desk, update the electronic copy.

There are many brands of PDA, and they're getting better. Your PDA should always be with you, and it should be synchronised with your desktop computer via a laser or docking station, whenever you return to your desk.

If the family needs you to be somewhere, teach them to put themselves into your diary.

 **Choose a diary system you enjoy using.**

Although electronic diaries (either desktop or handheld) are the most efficient, especially when you have synchronisation, many people don't like using them, and for lots of folk they are an unnecessary expense.

There are a number of reasons for this:

➡ An obvious one is that it will take another 20–30 years before most of the diehard non-computer souls will be an extinct race (at least in the workplace!). Don't be upset if you are one – we still love you.

➡ We all process information in different ways, and although most of us are a combination of several sensory preferences, we usually have one dominant one. The five major senses are visual (how things look to us), auditory (externally, how things sound, or internally, the sense and logic of the words), kinaesthetic (how something feels), olfactory (the smells associated with that item) and gustatory (taste).

➡ If you're strongly kinaesthetic, you won't feel comfortable unless you can feel your diary in your hand. You need to feel that you've 'got a grip' on things. Also, how it feels is important – you'll probably like the texture of a nice leather cover. If you're very visual the look is really important, and you need to be able to immediately see what's on. If you can't do this easily, you can neither think nor plan clearly. Of course, your diary can be handled with an electronic system, but it's got to look clear and attractive. Auditory people need to hear, or use the logic of words. Although electronic systems don't talk to you yet, the logic of the words is easy to access. Olfactory and gustatory processors are not so common, but if either of these is a primary method of anchoring information for you, computers definitely don't do it for you!

To transform the world into using electronic organisers is an uphill battle still. If you are part of a company where information has to be shared, I encourage you to persevere – it really will save heaps of time for everyone. However, look for ways and tools to accommodate your processing preferences as well.

9 Owl or fowl? Plan your day when you're sharp.

Some experts say plan first thing in the morning. Others say plan last thing before you leave work.

Who cares when you do it? The key thing is do it when you're fresh, when it suits you best, and when you get the best results.

Ask yourself, 'Am I sharp as a tack first thing in the morning, and do I do my best thinking then? Or do I need four cups of coffee before my brain switches on, but love working after everyone else leaves the office?'

If you are the former, maybe you're a fowl — if you've ever heard a rooster crow before dawn you'll know what I mean. You may find it challenging to plan the night before because your brain turns to mush by the end of the day. If you're an owl, functioning best at night, you'll do much of your best thinking then.

There are two main advantages of doing your planning the night before. Firstly, many experts say it is the best time as your subconscious can then work on anything that needs attention while you sleep. How often have you woken up with exactly the right answer in the forefront of your mind? Secondly, if you've done your 1–5 list the night before, as soon as you hit your desk the next morning you can get straight to work on the top priority.

If you're a fowl it would be smart to make notes throughout the day of anything relevant to the next day, on the next day's diary page. When you're ready to do your planning the next morning most things you need for your quick decision-making are there — your subconscious has been triggered to work on things overnight.

10 'No' is one of your most powerful time management tools.

So often we find ourselves taking on more than we can handle. It's not necessary to go to your grave with an inscription saying, 'Here lieth the one who couldn't say no. She died doing her duty.'

Every decision you make, every action you accept or agree to, signals a choice. Behind that choice is the multitudinous variety of other things that you now can't do, because of what you've just agreed to. Obvious as it seems, many people seem to forget that they really can do only one thing at a time.

Susan was called up by a neighbour to help co-ordinate a big community project. A busy mother of a large family, she needed another project like a hole in the head. However, not wanting to disappoint her friend, she reluctantly agreed. Having worked out the components of the job, she in turn picked up the phone and rang one of her girlfriends, confident that she'd help. Her friend said, 'Oh Susan, thanks so much for asking. I really appreciate your considering me, and I regard it as an honour. However, I have a number of deadlines I'm working on right now, and wouldn't be able to do a good job for you. I'll have to decline this time, but thanks again for asking, and I wish you all the best in finding someone to help.'

As Susan got off the phone she said to her family, 'I wish I'd thought of that!'*

---

* Stephen Covey, author of *7 Habits of Highly Effective People*, tells a similar story about his wife.

Get off the guilt trip many associate with saying no. It's okay. If you try and fit in more than is realistic, even if you achieve the seeming impossible, your health and your family will suffer. The higher your self-esteem the easier it is to say no to a request not aligned to your goals, to a request that breaks your concentration and focus.

Useful strategies
for
overcoming
procrastination

Key points

11 Chunk big tasks into smaller tasks — it makes the tasks less daunting.

12 Use a mind map for quick clarity.

13 Eat your vegetables first! Do the hard task first and the rest is a breeze.

14 Beware of majoring in minor things.

15 Develop a 'Do it NOW' attitude.

16 Start with the end in mind and mentally rehearse it. Thus, the end will be as you picture it.

17 Enjoy and celebrate every small milestone of success. This is a key tool for overcoming procrastination.

18 No time to work towards a big goal? Use the leftovers.

19 Enjoy creative procrastination. Put off until tomorrow that which won't advance your life-plan by being done today. Give yourself the gift of prime time to do whatever you like, including nothing!

20 Indecision is a thief of time — learn to weigh up the balance sheet of each situation quickly and get on with it. Only rarely does it really matter which way you go.

Chunk big tasks into smaller tasks — it makes the tasks less daunting.

Many of us beat ourselves up for procrastination, when all we need is better preparation. Consider these three 'chunking' strategies.

➡ **Chunk up** — identify the bigger elements of a task, looking for the bigger picture. Sometimes we get bogged down in minutiae, can't see the wood for the trees, and feel really stuck. A quick strategic overview will often show where your starting point needs to be. Ask yourself, 'What one thing, if I start there, is going to get this project moving? What is the critical point that will help everything else fall into place?'

➡ **Chunk down** — break large blocks of information into smaller, digestible snippets. Then you can easily focus your mind on the priorities that give the best impact. The daily 1-5 method discussed in Key Point 6 is a quick chunking method.

➡ **Chunk sideways** — clump like with like. Let's take today's mail. Sort it as if you were putting a pack of cards into suits. Make categories relevant to your work. They may include things like Internet research, email, writing or drafting information, phone calls, discussions with various individuals.

The activities won't all have equal value, but by separating categories into like with like, it's easier to see what needs to be done. It's also easier to stay focused on one task at a time.

 **Use a mind map for quick clarity.**

When you have a lot of ideas rattling around, a quick brain dump onto paper can turn that basket of cotton wool on your shoulders into the sharp brain you thought you'd lost at the supermarket.

The fastest way I know is to use some form of mind map. Some of you may be saying, 'I'm not clever with pictures' (especially if you've seen some of the really complex mind maps).

Relax, there are no rules. Words, lines, scribbles, stick pictures if you want graphics – anything goes. The point is that you can rapidly get a handle on the key elements of any situation in minutes. I use this process to plan speeches of an hour, workshops of two days, any complex project, and even books.

A4 paper is fine if you're on your own. Flipchart paper is great for a group. Below is a rough guide for how I do it, but the most important thing is that it has meaning for you.

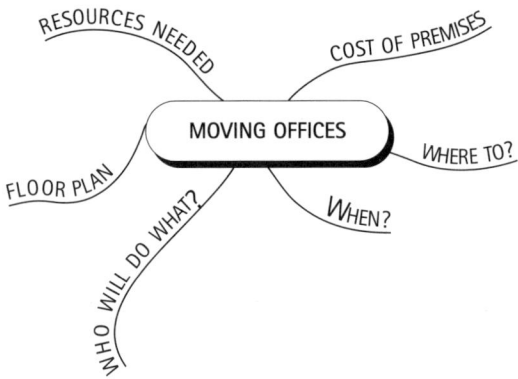

Once you've got your topic at the centre, and one key element of the topic per branch, it's time to go deeper. Once subsets of the topics start to come up, write them below the 'branches'.

If you've never done this before, you'll be surprised how quickly you glean the essence of a topic. The benefits, of course, are clarity, focus, and obvious first steps. You'll find yourself itching to get going, instead of wallowing in procrastination.

MIND MAPPING 101

 Eat your vegetables first! Do the hard task first and the rest is a breeze.

Ever procrastinated about something, even though you know it's important? By doing the most important task, or sometimes the hardest one, first thing in the day, we experience more job satisfaction, less stress, and we do a better job.

Think of the last time you dragged the chain on a tricky task, putting off something unpleasant, deferring deadlines, using side-stepping avoidance techniques that would make a football player envious. How did you feel? Heavy, lethargic, guilty sometimes, generally less than top class?

Conversely, ever noticed the rush of adrenalin when you finally tackle a task that's been hanging over your head for ages?

Learn to actively seek the feelings of success by taking action quickly. It releases endorphins, which make us feel more energetic. We're able to move faster and we get more done.

 **Beware of majoring in minor things.**

Simple tasks can easily seduce us into 'fiddling while Rome burns'.

Sometimes we find ourselves doing low-priority, low-value activities just to have a break. Or, we've moved up the business ladder but enjoy doing some of these routine activities, and don't really want to let go. The case may be that we haven't yet learnt how to delegate and train effectively.

Ask yourself, 'What hourly rate is this work worth?' If it's worth less than the rate you're earning, or can earn, look for ways to outsource or delegate it. While you do work that's worth a lesser amount, you're effectively earning that lower figure (or you're a very expensive resource to your organisation).

However, you also need to be aware of the benefits that you gain by involvement in the activity in question. If there is *some* value, perhaps there's a more efficient way to achieve it.

> The CEO of a middle-sized company enjoys helping to load the trucks at the factory door from time to time. He learns all kinds of useful information. The downside is that he works ridiculous hours to get his 'real' work done. He needs to decide which activities are the ones only a CEO can do, and how to efficiently receive the information gathered at the loading dock. It may be that a truck-loading session occurs from time to time and he gets more help with executive tasks.

Only the person in that position can assess the pros and cons. There is no simple answer.

 **Develop a 'Do it NOW' attitude.**

Interested in success? Winners get going – losers think about getting going. Every time you feel an 'I'll get round to it later' coming on, get your mental stockwhip out and refuse to allow yourself that lazy habit, for that's all it is.

It doesn't take very long to develop a sense of discomfort every time you find yourself slipping into procrastination, as long as you notice it and do something about it. That something may be very small. Every time you create a tiny win over a disempowering habit there's a sense of completion and accomplishment that builds the next infinitesimal block in the ladder of your success.

For instance, my friend John Vamos, CEO of Business Thinking Systems, a very successful franchise that helps businesses grow by the use of facilitated powerful and simple analysis tools, tells the following story about his tidy and well-run desk.

People often say, 'It's easy for you, John. It comes naturally to you.' I get really cranky when I hear that. What they don't realise is that I can never let up. Every day I have to push myself to achieve this state. The reason I do it is that I also know how it feels when it gets out of hand, and that's not a state I want to ever be in again.

Whatever hour God has blessed you with, take it with
grateful hand, nor postpone your jobs from year to year,
so that, in whatever place you have been,
you may say that you lived happily.

HORACE

Start with the end in mind and mentally rehearse it. Thus, the end will be as you picture it.

Something bogging you down? Imagine yourself at the other side of the event – successful, outcomes achieved, and feeling great.

This is part of a strategy called 'future pacing'. It comes from the behavioural science of Neuro Linguistic Programming (NLP), and helps prepare your mind for the successful outcome you want. Our minds are quite easy to train when we understand how they work.

Here's an example. Suppose you have to attend a business function. The standing-around, chatting-to-people stuff is not your cup of tea; you'd rather be at home with a good book. However, it's a new product launch for your department, and not attending would definitely be a career-limiting move. How can you turn a potentially uncomfortable situation into one you feel okay about?

You've got choices. One is to say, 'This will be awful, I don't want to be there, and no one will want to talk to me.' How will you come across to others as you talk to them? I suspect there won't be a lot of energy, enthusiasm, warmth and excitement in your voice, your posture or your body language. You've already talked yourself into a glum.

The other choice is to spend time rehearsing a better outcome.

➡ Imagine yourself after the event.

➡ See yourself leaving the room happy, talking animatedly to someone you've just met. Note the feelings of well-being, the glow of pleasure as you realise you've had a really interesting conversation with them.

➡ As you think about it, hold those feelings, sounds, pictures.

Build them into a strong mental video with full Technicolor effects.

➡ Then, mentally walk yourself backwards through all stages of the event, back to when you walked into the room at the start of the evening with positive anticipation.

Using this simple process gives your neurology a cellular memory of success. The fascinating thing is that the subconscious can't tell the difference between past, present and future. So, if you mentally rehearse a future success, when time catches up with the practice it feels comfortable and your actions will naturally follow the practice line.

This technique can be applied in any area of life, so why not try it with the next activity you're tempted to procrastinate on. See yourself smiling as you put away piles of paper, do your planning, get started on those big projects – whatever it is that you're currently allowing to run your life.

 **Enjoy and celebrate every small milestone of success. This is a key tool for overcoming procrastination.**

It constantly surprises me how few people really acknowledge their wins and successes. Many people are so busy looking forward, striving to reach their goals, that if you ask them what they've achieved they'll tell you what they have yet to do. Two things are happening here. First, they're future focused, and often don't think they're good enough yet. Now don't get me wrong – of course there's a place for that – it's an integral part of goal-setting and achievement.

However, every aspect of life has its light and dark side. If we spend all our time looking to the future, we miss the beauty and accomplishments of the now. And one of the things that often happens is that our subconscious gets rebellious. Support your subconscious by giving it success steps to anchor to. You'll find the next step easier. If all you do is beat yourself up for not succeeding, eventually you find yourself thinking, 'This is all too hard' – and you give up.

What about the last conversation you had with someone about their exercise or eating habits? Most folk will tell you they're not good enough (whatever that means for them). They'll tell you about how they slipped up, how they need to lose more weight.

Some years ago I worked for a woman named Mary. She came up with two clever ways to beat her procrastination about exercise. Firstly, she decided to use a little bit of our time together for exercise. My arrival became the trigger to go for a walk – it wasn't unproductive time: we did a vast amount of planning and strategising as we pounded the local footpaths. The other thing she did was draw up a 1–31 chart to reinforce the behaviour by setting some rewards.

How do you do a 1–31 chart? Take a piece of lined paper. Turn it on its side. Leave a column on the left large enough to write your task or tasks, and to the right of that draw 31 narrow columns for each day of the month. Number these columns – this is where you'll put the ticks as you achieve your daily targets. Not only do you write down your activity, but at the same time, decide how often you can realistically fit it into your month, and – very importantly – write down what reward you'll have when you achieve your targets.

TASK	1	2	3	4	5	6
Prospecting calls (5/day)		IIII	HHt ✓	HHt ✓	III	HHt ✓
Sales presentations (5/week)		✓	✓	✓		✓✓
Filing (3/week)		✓		✓		✓
Read business book (15 min/day, 4/week)					✓	
Exercise (3/week)	✓		✓			✓

I still remember, a month later, the deliciousness of sitting in a suburban picture theatre with Mary at 2 o'clock on a working day, eating ice cream. We felt like schoolgirls dodging school, and it was FUN!

No time to work towards a big goal? Use the leftovers.

So you haven't got time to write a book, or study for a qualification, or plan a new garden, or learn a musical instrument, or a new language, or acquire other new skills? Perhaps that's really true for you right now, but many don't utilise the gaps, the leftovers, the spaces in between other big tasks.

Stop and think for a minute. Who do you know, already successful in your chosen endeavour, that you could talk to?

You might like to ask them these questions:

➡ How much time did you devote to your goal on a daily or weekly basis?

➡ Were there always large blocks of time or did you also find ways to do small amounts of activity as you did other things?

The exception always proves the rule, but you will mostly find a large amount of goal-focused activity was done whenever an opportunity presented itself. Most successful people are superb at turning every spare moment to advantage.

Some suggestions (and use only what's relevant to yourself):

➡ On planes study, prepare, think or write.

➡ If you think you might be waiting for someone, take reading or study relevant to your topic.

➡ Turn driving into a learning opportunity using tapes. If you're a passenger you may choose to read and write instead.

➡ You spend a bit of time on hold for phone calls? Keep small tasks beside your phone that can easily be put down as soon as the caller comes on the line.

➡ When talking, listening or reading, engage a second level of attention that says to your brain, 'How can I turn this information into something of value?' Every interaction with others brings the opportunity to learn something new. You'll be able to write an article, or even a book, based on things you learn from others.

➡ What activities can you double up on? One of my clients really wanted to play more golf, *and* he wanted to spend individual time with his growing sons. He started taking his nine-year-old lad to golf with him when appropriate. The boy became good at golf and father and son developed a shared interest.

 Enjoy creative procrastination. Put off until tomorrow that which won't advance your life-plan by being done today. Give yourself the gift of prime time to do whatever you like, including nothing!

Procrastination is not all bad – there's good procrastination as well as bad! Learn to focus on the activities that lead you towards your goals and block out or procrastinate on the trivial, time-consuming minutiae. 'Stuff' (great word) is never going to go away.

My friend Mary Henderson, who with her husband Tony heads one of the biggest Amway businesses in the world, says, 'Will it make a difference in five years' time?' If it won't, she doesn't let the 'busy work' get in the way of enjoying life, family and friends. This has been Mary's philosophy right from the early days of her business, and a key part of her success.

Work the 80/20 rule to your advantage. After all, Pareto said that 20 percent of our activity would generate 80 percent of our results, and conversely 80 percent of our activity would generate only 20 percent of the results. Next time you think of keeping going, when your intuition tells you it's time to stop, ask yourself, 'What's important here?'

And what about this 'doing nothing' idea? Well-balanced people with healthy relationships and family lives know that time for themselves is also important, and just as vital as working productively and spending time with others. It's not selfish to give yourself quality time. In fact, I believe it is selfish not to, for someone who never takes time to recharge ceases to be effective in their other responsibilities.

 Indecision is a thief of time — learn to weigh up the balance sheet of each situation quickly and get on with it. Only rarely does it really matter which way you go.

Although every decision will have consequences and an impact on future events, with most it doesn't really matter which way you go, in the grand scheme of things. Only if something is critical should we make haste slowly. With the normal run of decisions to make, it is better to make your mind up and get on with it.

My daughter Catherine is a natural runner. In her senior school year the Membership Officer of a nearby athletics club saw her running in a school competition. Impressed, he invited her to become part of their club. She was very flattered to be asked. However, before making a final commitment she decided she'd give it a go for a few weeks to see if she could fit the training and meets into her schedule. I watched, increasingly concerned, as she struggled to fit athletics into her already bulging school, study and after-school activities. These included cleaning three houses to save money for a trip she had planned with one of her brothers.

For the duration of this experiment the family conversation was, 'Shall I, shan't I? Can I do it justice? If I do athletics, do I have to drop something?'

Eventually she made the decision to let it go — the whole thing was too hard. I was impressed with her mature approach to the whole exercise, but the thing that stood out in my mind was the enormous amount of time consumed in the decision-making process.

If she'd had enough experience to make that decision more quickly it would have saved her hours of time — time that would have been better employed on one or more of her higher priorities.

Working
efficiently
with
others

Key points

21 Delegation is a four-stage train journey, not a one-stop destination.

22 Set sensible deadlines, communicate them clearly, and give the staff member a chance to say whether they can perform to that deadline.

23 When you ask for something to be done by a specified date, let the person concerned know that you've noted their next action in your diary — it keeps them accountable.

24 Avoid that killer question, 'Do you understand?'

25 Once a person has a good grasp on a task, don't let them interrupt you with a question unless they also bring two possible solutions.

26 A good manager constantly looks for ways to make themselves redundant.

27 Praise releases energy, criticism kills it. Don't worry too much about what's not right — praise to the goal.

28 Once people understand the task, let them get on with it — they may have a better way. The most important point to communicate is the desired outcome.

29 If your boss keeps overloading you, give him or her a written list of your current tasks and ask which could be dropped off.

30 When receiving delegation from more than one source, let the people giving the instructions sort out scheduling conflicts.

 Delegation is a four-stage train journey, not a one-stop destination.

Delegation is a key skill for managers, but very few have formal training in it. Many lurch along, doing their best, often over-whelmed by their own work as well as the needs of their people, trying not to feel resentful at the time it takes to train others. Master this skill and you move into a new league — the exciting world of new horizons. You're free of the tasks that others, at a lower pay rate, lesser skill set, or with less responsibility can do as well as you.

There are four distinct stages in effective delegation, and if you don't step through each phase with the person you're delegating to, at some point you'll almost certainly have to backtrack. Master these four steps and you'll find yourself more patient during initial explanations, achieving better results faster. Yes, you could have done the job faster — at the beginning. However, it's a sure path to limiting your growth and success. Once you've trained someone properly you're free to move on to new challenges and opportunities.

The four stages are:

➠ **Directive behaviour by the delegator — high direction, low support.**
Initially a new person needs instruction, not the opportunity to use their initiative. You'll give them heaps of directions, and only a low amount of support in making decisions. They don't know enough to need much support.

➡ Coaching behaviour by the delegator – high direction, high support.

They are starting to understand the process. You encourage them to come to you with questions; you give plenty of explanations, and continue to instruct.

➡ Supportive behaviour by the delegator – low direction, high support.

These folk are starting to understand the process. You're weaning both you and them off lots of 'telling'. You now support them in making the decisions.

➡ Delegating behaviour by the delegator – low direction, low support.

Now you're free. Your delegatee not only has an excellent understanding of the task, but they have the confidence to get on with the job. They can still come to you for help if they need it, but that's a rare occurrence.

(This thinking is expanded in Kenneth Blanchard's excellent little book *Leadership and the One Minute Manager*, Fontana, 1987, new edition 2000.)

 Set sensible deadlines, communicate them clearly, and give the staff member a chance to say whether they can perform to that deadline.

This seems so obvious, but as with everything to do with human communication, the workplace is littered with examples of it done very poorly.

Some bosses put on their 'she who must be obeyed' air as they step out their front door each morning. They intimidate their staff to the point that it is only the very brave, very high self-esteem souls who would dare to suggest that they couldn't get something done. Thank goodness this management model is slowly dying! Such people never get the best out of their employees.

On the other hand, employees have a responsibility to communicate as well.

Susan, a senior manager with one of my air-freight clients, told the story of two staff members in her accounts team. Bill seemed to be the ideal employee. Whatever she asked of him, he willingly said, 'No problem, I can handle that.' He took all the work she gave him. She was most impressed. Laura, on the other hand, was quite an assertive person. If she felt Susan was overloading her, she was very quick to let her know. Many times Susan wished Laura was more like Bill, although she couldn't fault the work she did turn out.

One day Bill was away sick. They needed a file he was working on, so Susan had to dig into his desk. To her horror she uncovered a drawer full of unfulfilled promises, of late work, and of tasks procrastinated on.

The best employee is not necessarily the one who says the right things. Look for the one with the best productivity, and encourage them to tell you if they don't feel they can achieve a task within the required time. You're far better to know at the beginning. Then, with time to spare, you can either find another person, or renegotiate the deadline.

Sometimes the delegator will realise that the task wasn't that important anyway. Bosses often get enthusiastic about great ideas and forget what else they've already loaded on the willing packhorse next door!

When you ask for something to be done by a specified date, let the person concerned know that you've noted their next action in your diary — it keeps them accountable.

This can be done face to face or when you're issuing instructions over the phone. You can use it for staff, bosses, colleagues, and even clients. You can minute it in a meeting, make a note in your diary or, if you use an electronic system, you can simultaneously communicate a task and keep a record in your system. The options are varied. The key point is to let the other person know you're doing it. If you're on the phone, say, 'I'm just making a diary note to expect ... by ... Is that okay with you?'

> I was having a meeting with two partners of an accountancy firm. They had both identified themselves as 'challenged' in the arena of time management, and wanted their whole firm to be involved in an extended time management training programme. As we finished the briefing and agreed on dates, costs and all the usual details, Ray offered to send me some information. Without even thinking about the impact of my action I turned to the relevant spot in my diary and wrote a note to expect it. It arrived as promised.

We started the training a few weeks later. The group was discussing how to communicate expectations. To my surprise and amusement, Ray told his staff about this incident in our meeting.

> 'You folk know I sometimes forget to do things I've said I'll do', he said, 'but I have to tell you, when I saw Robyn write in her diary that by a certain date I would send her something, I knew I was in trouble if I didn't!'

There was a roar of laughter — we had all learnt a really important point.

And here's a bonus point. Ray knew the value of exposure. He's a very good manager, and not afraid to admit his weaknesses to his staff. Smart move — they know them anyway, and exposure brings respect.

So, this principle applies in all areas of life, including those concerning clients and prospects!

 **Avoid that killer question, 'Do you understand?'**

Get this phrase out of your vocabulary! Think about it for a moment. If someone asks, 'Do you understand?', what is the typical response? Only a handful of extremely high self-esteem souls will answer it truthfully if they don't quite have a grasp on the matter under discussion. Trouble is, it's a closed question, and leads the listener to either a 'yes' or a 'no'. If you've just given some instructions, they're still absorbing them. Their subconscious usually hasn't had time to check if there are any gaps in the information received, apart from the obvious. Most times it's not until we start a task that we realise there's more we need to know. And if we're the giver of the information, we're usually too close to it to realise we've left out a vital piece.

More useful questions are:

➥ I'm bound to have overlooked some details. What would you like me to go over again?

➥ You'll have some questions, I'm sure. What would you like to check on?

➥ I know that's a lot of information to take in at once. Go away, have a think about it, and come back in (and name a time that's convenient for you) with how you'll go about it, and any further questions.

➥ So, what do you think is the best way to start?

➡ What ideas spring to mind, or points that you would like to discuss further?

Another good strategy is to insist that people take notes of your instructions. Almost none of us, no matter how clever (unless we've had special memory training), can remember more than a maximum of nine pieces of information at a time, and for most of us this number can be reduced to three or five pieces of information (depending, of course, on their complexity).

I was running a meeting where one of the participants agreed to quite a number of actions. I began to get a little anxious when I realised she wasn't writing anything down. I knew from experience that she had a tendency to forget things. After the third action I said, 'Ann, would you like a pen and some paper?'

'Do you think I'll forget things, Robyn?' she said, a little defensive.

'Yes', was the honest answer. With no further discussion she took the paper, made the notes, and delivered on her promises!

 Once a person has a good grasp on a task, don't let them interrupt you with a question unless they also bring two possible solutions.

By nature, most of us will take the easy way. So, if someone you work with happily provides the answers to questions that might take you a minute or two to source, what are you constantly tempted to do? It's human nature to take the easy road, so why not ask – saves thinking!

If you, as a manager, find yourself constantly interrupted, your request to bring two possible solutions to every question rapidly gives you more time in the day – the little darlings soon realise that it's faster to do their own thinking and research! If you're too quick to supply the answer you encourage laziness and dependency.

One note of caution – link this technique to where the person is in the four delegation stages discussed in Key Point 21. In the directive phase they do need to be told everything, or nearly so. If you're in coaching mode you're still training them – invite them to come to you with their questions and some suggestions – you need to discuss with them what they think the answer might be. At this stage they still haven't enough knowledge or experience to automatically make the right decisions.

Once you move to the supportive phase they will be able to handle many things unaided. However, they still need some help. Require them to always submit potential solutions to any questions for discussion. It's at the delegating phase that this tip operates best.

A good manager constantly looks for ways to make themselves redundant.

Don't just delegate boring and repetitive work. Instead, consider how you can increase your staff's knowledge and skill base. If your staff are at least as good as you at a task, you're freed up to move to new opportunities.

Some people manage by withholding information. They operate from a fear motive – scared that the people under them might take their jobs. Wrong thinking. Any employee indispensable to an organisation, because they're the keeper of important knowledge that others don't have, is actually a threat to that company. If you see this happening, ask yourself, 'If this person leaves with all the knowledge they have in their head (or even goes on holiday), what will that do to our organisation?'

The impact on the other staff members when working with a withholder can show in several ways. They may sit back and not extend themselves. Their thinking is, 'If Joe wants to be a martyr, let him.' Joe gets burnt out: they have an easy ride.

The good ones often get very bored. If you see a department with a passing parade of staff, this is often the reason.

Resentment often swirls under the surface: people dislike restrictions. Discontentment can happen at any level – delegation is not just a management skill. A good manager makes sure that everyone is sharing learning opportunities with their fellow workers. A well-oiled machine always has more than one person who can step in and do a job.

Years ago, in my solo-parenthood days, struggling to make enough to feed and clothe my six children, I took on a part-time position as a teacher's aide in a school library, and was occasionally asked to assist the school secretary. I'd been out of the workforce for some years raising kids, and it was exciting to get back to my old career of librarianship, even at the princely sum of $7 per hour. (Despite the fact that I was seriously over-qualified for the job, I was really glad for the work.)

At the time electronic typewriters were quite new, and the office got one. It was so sexy! I'd learnt to type in my first library job, and ever mindful of the need to catch up with required workplace skills after eleven years away, suggested to the secretary that I'd love to learn. It was as if I'd offered to put poison in her children's food!

It took me a while to work out why she was so protective of the typewriter — she was afraid I'd pinch her job! She did me a favour. Determined to learn, I enrolled part-time at Community College. The exposure to new minds and thinking was a significant step in moving me to the wonderful life I now live.

 Praise releases energy, criticism kills it. Don't worry too much about what's not right — praise to the goal.

Praise and acknowledgement are the most powerful tools to an effective workplace. Very few people feel they're really recognised for their contributions. Good managers engender amazing loyalty by using it.

Whatever you focus on enlarges. When you praise to the skill you want the person to develop, their attention goes there. If you spend time telling them about the weak points, that's where the attention goes. If someone has done their best, and yet something isn't quite good enough, as long as it's not vital, just praise what they've done well. In a surprisingly short period of time you'll find their skill level has jumped amazingly.

The Toastmasters movement has nailed down this topic very well. Toastmasters is a huge international organisation, a voluntary group of people who help each other learn the art of speechcraft and polished public speaking. There's no room for criticism — if it were an unpleasant or uncomfortable group to belong to, no one would stay. They have a system to make sure that every speech, whether it be one or fifteen minutes, is constructively critiqued.

Human beings focus in on negative more than positive, and in order to overcome this we need to hear more praise than we do corrections. So Toastmasters use the acronym CRC — commend, recommend, commend — to anchor the process. I call it a praise sandwich. Take note — the word criticism is not there!

Here's an example:

'Well done, Jill. I like the way you moved briskly to the podium. You immediately had our attention with your lovely smile. You might like to look at changing the way you use your hands — perhaps a little too much gesticulation, but you'll find it quite easy to improve. Your content was excellent. You had our attention the whole time — I had to make quite an effort to remember to make notes for your feedback.'

Use your CRC to lubricate the self-esteem of your staff through great acknowledgement and appropriate feedback and you'll have no squeaky revolving doors as people leave in despair!

 Once people understand the task, let them get on with it — they may have a better way. The most important point to communicate is the desired outcome.

It's very tempting, especially when you're passing on a task that you used to do, to expect the next person to do that task exactly as you used to. After all, you know what works and what doesn't. You've made your mistakes and you want to save them the angst of unnecessary wasted time. That's fine — at the beginning.

However, once they understand the basic process, and more importantly, have a good comprehension of the desired outcomes, leave them to find the method that's best for them. Often they'll surprise you and come up with improvements.

Who do you want as an employee — someone who comes in excited at discovering new and better ways of doing things, or someone who leaves their brain parked at the door, does time, and then on the way home picks up their brain again?

 **If your boss keeps overloading you, give him or her a written list of your current tasks and ask which could be dropped off.**

A radio station manager was constantly overloaded by his general manager. I suggested that he make a list of his current tasks and display it where the boss could see it. He chose the whiteboard on the wall.

The next day his boss came in, ready to enthusiastically part company with the latest crop of good ideas (a common habit of bosses – we don't mean to overload, but once a task has gone it tends to sink to the bottom of our memory bank).

Paul pointed at his whiteboard, and also showed his boss his diary, full of appointments with sales reps and suppliers. He then politely asked, 'Which things would you like me to shift in order to do these new things?'

His general manager took a startled look at this amazing example of well-planned organisation and, muttering under his breath, retreated with the pile still in his hands.

 When receiving delegation from more than one source, let the people giving the instructions sort out scheduling conflicts.

Staff sometimes find themselves in the middle of a war zone, pushed and pulled by the demands of people more senior than themselves and with more work than they can realistically do.

Depending on their confidence level, many feel that the best way to handle the situation is just work harder, stay back, miss lunch, do whatever they have to do, in order to meet the deadlines imposed. Another variation on the theme is to put the work of the strongest personality at the top, because they make the most noise if their work isn't done.

Neither of these is a very attractive long-term strategy. Problem is, if you let these probably quite well-meaning people get away with overloading you, that's the standard you've set. They'll then expect you to keep working at burnout levels to try and accommodate them. Direct the problem back to its source.

Suppose you're working on a report for Jim. He needs it first thing in the morning. He's been organised, given it to you in plenty of time, and you're right on schedule to deliver. You look up and there's Ann with a rush job in her hand. Don't just accept Ann's last-minute task. Tell Ann your deadlines for the other work, and if she can't wait, ask her to discuss it with Jim. If it really is as urgent as she says, sometimes there is someone else in the office who can help.

Here's a further tip when dealing with a regular last-minuter. By always dropping what you're doing to accommodate that person

you encourage poor planning behaviour. Warn the person that you won't be able to continue the practice, and next time it happens refuse to take it on. Even if the person ends up embarrassed in front of someone else, that's not your problem; it belongs entirely to the last-minuter!

General time management strategies

Key points

31 Interruptions are insidious. Each small one invisibly slashes the concentration of all parties concerned. Save them for the next appropriate break and don't interrupt yourself or others with only one question or topic.

32 Create a Red Time/Green Time culture in your organisation which gives everyone at least one hour of uninterrupted time per day.

33 When seated at your desk, where do your eyes look? Try changing your view and you may well suddenly find another hour a day!

34 Keep traffic areas for walking, work stations for working — look for ways to separate the two.

35 Beware the electronic income-reducer — alias the television set. It has an 'off' switch — use it frequently.

36 If every day you become 1 percent better at at least one regular activity, the only thing that stands between you and your success is time.

37 If you can identify a person's preferred communication method you're more likely to get their attention.

38 Are you a last-minuter, often arriving stressed and flustered at your destination? Remember that 'one last thing' you squeezed in before you left, thinking you were being efficient? DON'T DO IT.

39 Get ready early — and then do the 'other' things.

40 In order to go faster, first you must go slower.

Interruptions are insidious. Each small one invisibly slashes the concentration of all parties concerned. Save them for the next appropriate break and don't interrupt yourself or others with only one question or topic.

Take your mind back to the last time you were engaged in a big and important task. I bet at some stage you interrupted yourself. You noticed an important idea slipping past the corners of your mind and you had to catch it by the coat tails or it would vanish. Or someone you needed to speak to walked past your desk. Almost before you realised it you found yourself talking to your colleague, or on the phone, the Internet, or down the corridor. The Very Important Task lay languishing on your desk.

Five, ten or thirty minutes later you look at your desk again, shake your head, and try to remember what you were up to.

Familiar? It is for most people. And we wonder why we frequently feel so frustrated staying back late to get the 'real' work done. Staff do it to bosses and each other, bosses do it to their staff.

The reason we jump when the idea sneaks in is that we think we'll forget it if we don't tend to it immediately. That's true, but that action does not need to be an interruption. Try one of these simple techniques to handcuff your self-induced thieves.

Have a piece of paper beside you, but just out of eye-range. Jot that passing thought down and you can, with confidence, go back to the task in hand.

Make the action a quick note on your 'To Do' list.

If it's someone you report to, or who reports to you, have a coloured manila folder in your desk file drawer with their name on it, whip out the file, jot down the note, and put it back until a pre-arranged meeting time.

If one of your colleagues is an interrupter, ask them to save their queries and give them a time you'll be free. The really bad ones can't help themselves — refuse to talk to them, remind them of your request, and keep working.

Here's an example of how to handle self-interruptions:

As I write this book, something I write triggers other things I want to tell you, or a better way I could describe a point. If I stop then and find the place to insert the little visitor, I'm likely to be sidetracked, and most importantly, I lose the flow of the current section. I keep a piece of paper beside me, quickly jot the idea down, and at my next natural break, scroll through the pages to find the best place to insert it.

 **32** Create a Red Time/Green Time culture in your organisation which gives everyone at least one hour of uninterrupted time per day.

Just for a moment, think how it would feel if you could have some uninterrupted time every day. When I ask my audiences about this they usually look at me with longing, and answers like 'pure gold' are bounced back.

The open plan environment that so many people work in these days has its benefits – but it also has major drawbacks. The worst is the ease with which staff can have their concentration broken. Even telling someone you're busy has broken your train of thought. The easiest way to indicate your interrupt/non-interrupt status is to have a signal visible on approach (a bit like an airport runway!).

You might like to try the following technique. A number of large corporate companies use it, including some branches of American Express and Lion Nathan.

➡ Issue everyone with a set of red and green flags (see our website: **www.gettingagripontime.com** to order sets for your office).

➡ When you don't want to be interrupted pop the red flag (fasten it with Blu-Tac) on the top of your computer.

➡ When you're busy but it's okay to talk, exchange the red flag for the green flag.

A few key points to ensure success. This technique is fun, easy, and very effective. However, it's rapidly destroyed if you're not firm, or if you don't get buy-in from the whole team. Stagger the times your team is on red time, and get people to cover each other, as you would for lunch. Divert the phone for that time, or put it on voice mail. If you're lucky enough to have a door, shut it. Handle things you know are likely to be important interruptions before you start, and as soon as you come off your red time, quickly deal with anything that's come up. Otherwise, if people have to wait too long they'll get frustrated and will not be prepared to play the game.

Other alternatives to the flags are:

➾ a red cap,

➾ a red cloth over the back of your chair,

➾ a piece of red paper taped on your door,

➾ a signal that the rest of the team recognise (one of my clients uses soft toys, the upside-down teddy bear means 'I'm busy'),

➾ or a PA who threatens to shoot intruders if they dare to interrupt (for senior people with that support).

Have fun with it, but DO it.

**When seated at your desk, where do your eyes look?
Try changing your view and you may well suddenly
find another hour a day!**

An Information Technology (IT) manager in a large bookselling
franchise was overwhelmed with too much to do, or so it seemed.
I discovered that his desk faced swinging doors, right beside
reception. At a rough guess, at least a hundred times a day those
doors opened and someone walked through. The answer was
simple. He swung his desk around to face away from the door,
positioned some bookshelves to block the view, and was delighted
at the extra hours he gained and the dramatic reduction of
interruptions. His work requires lots of concentration, but being
the nice man he is, every time someone came through the door
the temptation was to lift his head and make eye contact.

Once eye contact is established you give a person unspoken permission to interrupt, at the least breaking *your* concentration. If
you can't shift your desk, perhaps you can use pot plants or a
screen, or persuade the company to have higher screens for the
partitions. Desks side by side and face to face might save the
company floor space, but I guarantee you they won't increase
production. Vast amounts of invisible money will be wasted every
day because some people cannot work effectively in that
environment. The best partitions allow the worker some privacy
and a bit of sound-break while sitting, without being so high that
you have to walk around to see if they're at their desk.

Keep traffic areas for walking, work stations for working — look for ways to separate the two.

Following on from Key Point 33, what else is going on in each area of the office? Who regularly comes past and interrupts the people sitting there?

Inefficient seating plans are everywhere! I've seen senior people in narrow spaces that everyone walks past on the way to the kitchen; a researcher sitting next to a photocopier; a photocopier that served a large accounting office located at the far side of the room where one had to pass ten people to reach it.

In the last instance, as soon as the copier was moved nearer the middle of the room the interruptions dropped dramatically and productivity jumped.

It's easy to forget that just because you've got a minute to chat whilst the copier does its thing, the person you're interrupting doesn't. They've probably had ten people in the last twenty minutes doing exactly the same!

And, surprise, surprise, we have different levels of tolerance to noise. If someone needs quiet to work, don't put them in heavy traffic areas. Where possible, try to match the seating arrangements with the processing style of the person who'll sit there.

If you know you are negatively influenced by other people's noise, negotiate to have your desk moved. One engineer realised that too much noise from other people was incredibly distracting for him. He found a back corner, as far away from the front door as he could get, and moved his desk behind a screen.

However, not everyone will take responsibility for their own environment. If you're in charge of staff, be aware of how often you see people wasting time. The PA of the general manager of an advertising company loved a chat. By seating her where everyone else walked past to get to their desks they automatically ensured that both she and the general manager were dissatisfied. It became a case of 'move her or fire her'!

Beware the electronic income-reducer — alias the television set. It has an 'off' switch — use it frequently.

Everything in life has a positive and negative side, so I'm sure you're not surprised to hear me include television in the list.

Please don't get me wrong — I agree that television has many very important benefits. There are some wonderful educational programmes, it's a terrific way to relax, and it brings sports events to the world that we would otherwise only dream of attending.

However, beware of the dark side! Television is a passive occupation, and none know it better than the people who work in the industry. My friends at Television New Zealand inform me that vast amounts of research show that the more television you watch the slower your brain cells function.

Brian Tracy, author of the book *Maximum Achievement* and many wonderful training programmes, says that the more television you watch, the less able you are to make a really good income. Reason? While you're receiving other people's ideas you're not creating your own original ones. Nor are you expanding your abilities or horizons, except in a passive way.

Monitor your viewing patterns. Time yourself and see just how many hours you spend in front of the box. Don't turn it on as soon as you get home. Get it out of the lounge and put it in a small room somewhere else (if your house can accommodate that). Plan to have at least some nights where you don't eat in front of it (my recommendation is never to eat in front of it, but that might be too radical for some!). Save small tasks to do during the ads. Decide, as a family, how many programmes you really want to watch, and as soon as they're done, switch it off.

When my children were young, I realised that the tube was dominating our house and I was breeding a tribe of couch potatoes. After a family discussion, they agreed to limit the daily quota of television to two choices per child. The challenge came when trying to fit in the programming choices of six children! Solution? They didn't play in the lounge if it wasn't their show. There were bedrooms, the garage, the garden, and the nearby beach to play in.

I'm so glad of that decision. As adults none of them is wedded to the screen, and they've all made exciting career choices.

36 If every day you become 1 percent better at at least one regular activity, the only thing that stands between you and your success is time.

Develop a mindset of continuous improvement. As long as it's done in a positive way, accepting of where you already are, you're onto a winning formula. However, a big warning: sometimes people get so fixated on the goal that they forget to enjoy the journey. Beware of beating yourself up because you haven't reached the giddy heights you're aspiring to – that's a seriously useless exercise in self-flagellation, and as useless as tits on a bull (showing my country origins here)!

We have a wonderful role model in Ben Franklin. Although his formal schooling ended at age ten, he was committed to continuing his education. His next step was to study arithmetic at night. At age twelve, he added formal writing exercises. In his teens, he added foreign languages including French, Italian, Spanish and Latin. He achieved outstanding success as a scientist, inventor, statesman and writer, and in a relatively short number of years moved from poverty to great wealth. Today, millions of people's lives are better because of his inventions (bi-focal glasses being one of them).

One of Franklin's secrets was his system of self-evaluation, not of his academic skills but of his attitudes and behaviour. For most of his adult life he ran a scoring system based on twelve key attributes including temperance, honesty, virtue and timeliness. (If you can find a copy of his autobiography you'll get a full description.) Had you frisked his pockets you would have found a little notebook with a grid pattern of lines on every page. Also

listed was the one behaviour he wanted to focus on that week. As the day progressed a sequence of dots, based on his own code, indicated how he scored himself.

As an old man he described his young self as self-opiniated, lacking in true friends, and obnoxious to the people he admired. His scoring system enabled him to change that, small step by small step, until he became one of the most famous and admired men of his age.

If you can identify a person's preferred communication method you're more likely to get their attention.

Ever noticed that it has become increasingly difficult to get the attention even of existing clients who want to be communicated with! My friend Terrie Anderson, who works at very senior executive levels in IT, offers a very smart observation. Find out how people like to be communicated with – face to face, phone, fax, or email – and you're much more likely to be noticed.

The new Human Resources Manager of one of my clients asked me to contact him on a certain date. I'd done a considerable amount of work for them, they were very happy with the results, and discussions had been afoot for the next round before a change in personnel. At the pre-arranged date I rang. A few days later I rang again, I left it a week or so, and called again; and again (all this spread over about two months)! I couldn't work out what was going on, put it down to the new man still shaking down into a very demanding job, and left it a while. However, I was getting a little concerned. How often do we lose a good client because a new person, with whom you don't have the relationship, chooses another supplier? Then, just on a fluke, I tried an email.

'Dear John, not sure if my messages are being delivered, but just wanted to touch base as you'd requested. Thought that perhaps it might be easier for you to respond to email. How's the planning going for the next time management course?'

Within a day, back came this reply: 'You're right; you've got my attention now! We're not ready yet, but thanks for making the effort to keep in touch, and we'll talk soon.' Subsequently, we worked together on a very large staff training project.

 Are you a last-minuter, often arriving stressed and flustered at your destination? Remember that 'one last thing' you squeezed in before you left, thinking you were being efficient? DON'T DO IT.

We broadly fit into one of two styles when it comes to processing time. We're either in-time or through-time. The in-timers, bless their socks, are great at being fully present, totally in the moment (which is why this style is called in-time, not because they're punctual!), but challenged at getting to places or completing tasks on time. For them, it seems efficient to fit in 'one more thing' – to get somewhere early is to waste time. You'd wonder why the stress they suffer doesn't change their behaviour. They seem to suffer permanent memory loss on the topic. Most of it is caused by that 'one more thing' they squeezed in!

Through-timers, on the other hand, are more objective: they are able to detach, to see themselves outside of the events they're involved in. They seem to be effortlessly punctual. Their ability to easily see 'through' or along a time continuum makes it automatic for them to estimate how long they'll need for any activity.

For each style, their strength is also their weakness. Opposites often attract; they tend to drive each other nuts until they learn to play to their strengths and support the other's weakness.

An in-timer's skill is being fully present and focused on what they're doing. The downside is that they find it hard to extract themselves and forward plan. It can be done. I'm one, but I can never completely relax on it.

Punctuality doesn't come naturally to me. (I reward myself for good behaviour now and then by reverting to type when it doesn't matter!)

A through-timer's strength is their ability to detach, keep focused on the 'main' thing, and to be aware of the passage of time and its consequences. On the other hand, this same skill can mean they are perceived as being abrupt. They have to work harder to ensure that they're not seen as disinterested.

Apart from the tip at the beginning of this Key Point, another useful technique is to start with the end in mind. Count back approximately how many minutes you need for each step of the way, until you arrive at the beginning. Typically, you'll go, 'That's ridiculously early. I'll be sitting around waiting!' You won't, you know. You'll just be less stressed. However, always take a useful task to do on arrival, just in case.

Most in-timers have become A1 graduates at blocking the subconscious on this issue. They only notice it as a fleeting moment of discomfort, and then they push the awareness aside.

Solution: start listening!

39 Get ready early — and then do the 'other' things.

This follows through from the previous point. So many of my students are struggling and frustrated in-timers, and need all the help they can get. Poor dears — I really do understand!

Going somewhere? Get ready first and then go back to the other jobs you thought you could fit in. Once you're on the road, get to your destination before you stop for breaks. Find the place you're heading to, and then have the coffee or do the little fill-in tasks.

As I've told you, I am naturally an in-timer. I've had to be very conscious of these seemingly simple matters in order to stop embarrassing myself. Even in my early days of being a time management specialist I still sometimes tripped over myself.

This next story dates back a good few years now. At the time I was getting better at the 'get there first and then relax' system, but God must have decided I needed a further 'experience' to consolidate the learning!

I was booked to run an after-school programme for the staff of a city school, in a suburb I didn't know very well. I set out in plenty of time, crossed the Harbour Bridge, and, thinking I was only five minutes away from the school, parked beside the harbour to enjoy the spare fifteen minutes I thought I had. Then, relaxed and rested, I headed off.

The sense of peace and tranquillity didn't last long!

Imagine my dismay as I crawled through an unfamiliar long, skinny suburb to the far end, hampered by the afternoon discharge of dawdling chattering children from five other schools,

and every mother and child in the city slowly meandering their way to the major shopping centre just along the road. Red-faced, stressed out, and acutely embarrassed, I arrived at my destination to find a roomful of teachers waiting for me.

It's not a real good look to be late for your own time management course!

 In order to go faster, first you must go slower.

How many times do we hear people say 'I haven't got time to ...'? Many times it's true, but if you notice yourself repeatedly using this phrase, step back a bit and analyse what it is you're referring to.

What are you really saying? You haven't got time to teach someone else? You haven't got time to improve a regular process? You haven't got time to create a new product, or system, or new market (or whatever is relevant to your occupation)?

Wrong thinking. You can't afford not to take the time. If you always defer the long-term for the urgency of the short-term you will never grow, improve, and step into the next stage of your own success and the richness that life is waiting to offer you.

Every change requires a step back, a slowing down. In fact, I'd be very suspicious of the effectiveness of anyone who swings into a new task without a parallel reduction of speed. How much thinking have they done? What effort has gone into looking for the most efficient way of performing the task? Welcome each new challenge, accept that it will slow you down for a little while, and look forward to the increase in productivity and new opportunities once you've mastered it.

Managing
the
phone

Key points

41 Whether the caller or receiver of a phone call, start as you mean to go on.

42 Use a headset.

43 Learn to use the fast-dial and other time-saving features on your phone, both desk and mobile. If on hold, use the speaker until the other party answers, or a headset, so you can keep working.

44 When you're having Red Time (see Key Point 32), have your phone diverted. A ringing phone is very hard to ignore.

45 Don't take calls when you've got someone in your office — ever (unless it's an absolute crisis). If you're at the receiving end of this poor management skill, be proactive — educate your boss.

46 If you tend towards the garrulous, try watching time slip through the hourglass of your life — place an egg timer on your desk.

47 Stand up when you take a call — you'll be faster.

48 Chunk your phone calls together. It's faster to do a bundle of calls, one after the other, than to spread them randomly through the day. This creates a sense of urgency and helps you keep them short and effective. It also helps you get more calls handled in the day, if that's part of your role.

49 When you can't reach someone, leave a detailed message and let them know when you're available. On your message service, ask the caller to leave a detailed message, their phone number, and to speak slowly.

50 Before you call someone, have a mini-agenda prepared. This saves a call back because you've forgotten something.

47 Whether the caller or receiver of a phone call, start as you mean to go on.

A courteous 'How can I help you?' or 'What can I do for you today?' within the first few seconds of a conversation helps to focus the caller. Otherwise you're liable to find yourself in three or four minutes of 'how's your father' conversation, with nothing to show for it but an escalating workload. Many people feel they have to be chatty before they can get to business. Of course, chat has a very important place in building relationships, but it may not be appropriate today. If you're happy to hear from your caller, but want to cut to the chase, take control.

You're on a tight deadline? Try something like, 'Hi, I've only got a few minutes, but glad you rang. How can I help you?' People appreciate being given the parameters at the beginning. There's nothing worse than finding out, five or ten minutes into a conversation, that the person on the other end has a pressing deadline and you won't be able to get a conclusion to your call.

You've initiated the call? Try something like this:

'Hi, Jim, it's great to catch up. I know how busy you are, so I'll be brief. I've got three things to discuss with you, and it will take about five minutes. Have you got time to talk right now, or would you prefer me to call back at a later time?'

Courtesy is shown, you've given the framework, and you've asked permission to talk. Most busy people appreciate this kind of phone call.

 Use a headset.

This simple, inexpensive piece of equipment should be compulsory for anyone who uses the phone a lot and needs to type or write notes at the same time. How many times have you seen someone, phone tucked between shoulder and ear, back hunched, scrummaging around their desk looking for something? Such behaviour is very bad for your back and long-term health.

Once you get used to a headset, male and female, senior executive as well as front-desk receptionist, you'll never want to go back to a handheld phone at your desk. Quite aside from the posture issue, you can do so much while your hands are free – stand up and reach for something a couple of paces away, filing, enter details on your computer, keep working while you're on some of those interminable holds – the benefits are legion.

Some phone systems may not accommodate a headset, but even if you have to invest in new equipment to support them, I strongly believe they're worth every penny. I was forced to buy one for a telemarketer some years ago. She didn't do a very good job of the telemarketing, but I shall be forever grateful to her for the legacy of the headset. It's saved me hours of time.

I don't wear it all the time; it sits just beside my phone. Whenever the phone rings I quickly pop it on before I take the call, for nine times out of ten something needs to be written down, usually in our contact management system.

Watch for the following indicators that show a headset is needed:

➡ Staff constantly jotting notes on scraps of paper, and then losing them.

➡ Intermittent or spasmodic recording of important information.

➡ Information recorded twice, once on a piece of paper and then later in the permanent record.

➡ People doing nothing while they wait on hold – for ages.

➡ People with a phone sandwiched between shoulder and ear, a tight neck and shoulder muscles and a sore back.

 Learn to use the fast-dial and other time-saving features on your phone, both desk and mobile. If on hold, use the speaker until the other party answers, or a headset, so you can keep working.

Monitor yourself and your staff. How much time is spent redialling, looking up regularly used numbers, keying in frequently called numbers or examining your fingernails while you listen for the tenth time to 'We appreciate your call, you will be answered by the next available operator'?

In your dreams you hang up and leave them customerless. Trouble is, often it's the bank, the IRD, a critical service provider you absolutely have to speak to, or some terribly important client.

So, get smart. Work on something else near the phone while technology does the 'hold' work for you.

Here's a great bonus tip from my bookkeeper. One morning, when she realised that a call to the IRD would be necessary, she put the call through as soon as she arrived at the office. If you call first thing in the morning to these kinds of places, you often get through with little or no wait.

When you're having Red Time (see Key Point 32), have your phone diverted. A ringing phone is very hard to ignore.

If noise distracts you easily you'll find your good intention not to pick up your phone is easily discarded. Or, you may be part of a company whose culture is to answer all calls with a 'real' person (loud cheers from your callers!). If you don't have a secretary or receptionist who can take the calls while you're on Red Time, see if you can set up a shared arrangement with a colleague. They're bound to appreciate it when you return the favour.

Be sure to coach whoever is taking your calls on how you want your messages handled. You don't want variations on, 'Sorry, she's not taking calls just now.' Try something like 'I'm sorry, Sue is unavailable right now', or, 'Bill is in a meeting at the moment, I'm sorry. (You are in a meeting – with yourself!) However, he will be available again at ... o'clock. When will you be available for him to return your call?'

If you work in a situation where none of the options above is possible, and for some reason you can't programme your phone to go straight to voicemail without you having to listen to it, how about diverting to your mobile? Have a suitable message, and then switch it off.

Be sure to get straight back to people when you surface again.

 Don't take calls when you've got someone in your office — ever (unless it's an absolute crisis). If you're at the receiving end of this poor management skill, be proactive — educate your boss.

I am constantly amazed at the number of senior executives who take calls when they're having a meeting, formal or informal, with staff. They seem to have a non-existent courtesy filter, and a total blind spot about the cost to the company of keeping experienced people standing around.

If you're guilty of this behaviour, do some sums. Count not only the hourly rates you're costing the company by having others twiddle their thumbs (while you rabbit on to someone else), but also the lost opportunity cost.

Here are some ideas for you to try if your boss is a consistently guilty party:

➡ Say, as you walk into a meeting with them, 'Shall I get the receptionist to hold our calls?'

➡ You can probably handle one quick call. However, if it keeps going, let them see you looking at your watch.

➡ If that doesn't work, write them a note along the lines of, 'I'm at my desk when you're ready', or, 'I'm sorry, I have to go. We'll have to reschedule', and walk out.

➡ If they complain because you've walked out, it's time to be straight up with them. Maybe they've never thought about the consequences of their behaviour. Sometimes you come across egomaniacs who think no one else's time is as important as theirs — that may be true but it's not the point!

A good manager is profit-driven. Before you head into education mode with your boss, it could be useful to time-log how much time you spend waiting. Work out the cost to the company of your wasted time, in dollars. Also, list projects awaiting attention. Then give him or her a cost/benefit analysis.

I'm not suggesting mutiny – I am encouraging efficient use of everyone's time.

If you're a salesperson you may be thinking, 'That's all very well, but what if the person taking calls is a client?' You have to make a decision based on all the factors (including your own confidence levels), but if you're prepared to make a stand, a variation of the same techniques can still work. I've known of top salespeople who, after the third interruption, have said to the client, 'It seems that now is not a very good time. When can we reschedule that will give us uninterrupted time?'

On the other hand, sometimes you decide to grin and bear it. I can think of one client who does this to me. His office calls are usually held, but he leaves his mobile on nearly all the time. The upside is, he's very hard to pin down in the office but I know I can almost always get him on his mobile if I've got a quick question – and he's interrupting someone else!

 If you tend towards the garrulous, try watching time slip through the hourglass of your life — place an egg timer on your desk.

There's a particular personality style that will find this idea useful. You're a friendly outgoing soul, you love to catch up with people, and you absolutely know that the best business is done with people who like you. If you could find a way to be paid for chatting, you'd die a happy camper!

If you're also an in-time person (see Key Point 38) and a visual processor of information, you'll be helped by a visible reminder of just how long you've talked. The fact that time is passing hardly makes a ripple on your conscious mind.

Go out and buy the most outrageous egg timer you can find. Every time the phone rings, start it. A few weeks of use and you'll have developed a better sense of appropriate phone time, then you can bequeath it to your most talkative friend!

On a less flamboyant note, many modern office phones have a digital clock display. You might like to get into the habit of jotting the time down as you pick up the phone. (If you're in an industry that requires tight time-keeping you'll already have that habit.) Challenge yourself and pretend you're in a call centre where they monitor call-times very tightly. Set yourself small mini-goals to handle each call in a certain number of minutes, and enjoy something delicious as a reward — chocolate fish or jelly beans usually go down well!

47 Stand up when you take a call — you'll be faster.

When we're on our feet we tend to speak more quickly, we have a higher level of energy, and we move more quickly. Play to this when wanting to get through calls quickly.

Think of a phone call as a meeting down a phone line (you can use the same strategy for meetings). There's no forward momentum when we're sitting down. We tend to relax, settle into our seats, our voices often reflect our posture, and the whole conversation slows down a notch or two.

Here's another angle. You may have conducted most of the call in your seat, and you want to draw it to a close. Stand up. Your change in posture will be reflected in your voice, and most callers will get more of a sense of speed. (The unobservant ones may need to be prompted, but you'll find it extra easy to hurry them up once your shoe leather is on the carpet.)

48 Chunk your phone calls together. It's faster to do a bundle of calls, one after the other, than to spread them randomly through the day. This creates a sense of urgency and helps you keep them short and effective. It also helps you get more calls handled in the day, if that's part of your role.

Ever noticed the speed with which you can process a stack of calls when you come back into the office? The momentum is artificially created by the concentration of the task. It's easy to create that same impression of speed and push ourselves to a more productive level by batching calls together.

When do we process the requests generated by those calls? Even though there is a nice feeling from completing each item before we move on to the next call, in this case I don't recommend it, unless it can be done quickly with resources right at your fingertips. If you process as you go, you may find yourself sidetracked before you've completed the ringing and talking.

You're in sales? Effective salespeople maximise phone time. Ineffective ones, often without realising it, look for excuses to get off the phone. Suppose their target is ten new calls per day (a not unreasonable quota), and they have only an hour to do them. They make a call, are asked to send out some information, and suddenly they're stuffing literature in envelopes or running something off the computer. Most of the other nine calls sit patiently in the file, wondering when they'll be noticed. If the manager asks, this kind of salesperson can, in total truth, say, 'There wasn't enough time to get to the other calls; the first couple generated too much work.'

Use commercial hours for direct contact. If you're building a business, increasing your sales, or generally working to lift your productivity, save the paperwork for the times of the day when you're less likely to reach the person on the other end of the phone.

When you can't reach someone, leave a detailed message and let them know when you're available. On your message service, ask the caller to leave a detailed message, their phone number, and to speak slowly.

Telephone tag can be fantastically useful, and terribly frustrating; either a huge time-saver or an enormous time-waster. Which camp it falls into depends on the skill of both the phone owner and the caller, and the quality of the information asked for and left.

Always leave as much information on a message as is appropriate. Try something like, 'You've reached Bill Bloggs' phone, and I'm sorry, I'm not able to take your call. If you leave your phone number, a detailed message and when you're available, I'll be ready to help you when I return your call.'

There is one detail that many people trip up on, and it's guaranteed to drive most of us to frustration. Ever received a message where the caller gabbles their phone number at the end of a long-winded story, and you have to play it over four times to try and get the number? And if you're on your mobile you're paying for the privilege of listening to their dulcet tones, over and over! I've finally fixed it by educating the caller on my voicemail message. Try something like the message above, and add '... and please say your number slowly'.

Now, if you're a salesperson you may not be sure about leaving messages. Of course, you don't want to spoil your 'pitch'. Perhaps it's better not to leave a message, and to call back in the hope of getting your prospect at their desk. I have to tell you, with voicemail and the sheer overload of communication methods these days, that chance is getting slimmer!

I once worked for Murray Thom, a very successful New Zealand businessman. He told us how he used to get through to prospects, leaving messages when he needed to, without annoying them or spoiling his opportunity.

'Most people give up after one or two attempts to get through to a prospect. They think, probably correctly, that the person doesn't want to talk to them. Instead, leave a polite and brief message, something like, "Murray Thom called, and sorry to miss you. My number is ... and I'll call back in a day or two if we miss each other." As long as you're always courteous, by the time you get through the person you are calling can feel as if they almost know you purely from the spaced repetition of the messages. You can easily insert a bit of humour and you'll find it easy to swing into the conversation. You've also probably built up a relationship with the secretary or receptionist if they have one — always a useful resource!'

Before you call someone, have a mini-agenda prepared. This saves a call back because you've forgotten something.

Unless you've got only one thing to discuss with someone, make notes of the topics under discussion before you call. I use my diary to jot things down. If it's an important call, or one we've scheduled to happen at a set time (a meeting by phone), I've usually started the list before the day of the call.

> One of my book and tape distributors, a very organised chap in a distant city, used email to set the agenda and the time of a call. Then, four days before the call, I was most impressed to receive not only the agenda, but also his preliminary thoughts on points he wanted in-depth discussion on. Although the call was reasonably lengthy (there were many things to discuss), we were both fully prepared. We had a very focused and useful conversation, and nothing was left out. It is an absolute pleasure doing business with him.

Often you make a quick call and the person is not available. Even if you didn't have an agenda beforehand, as you leave the message take a moment to jot down the matter you wanted to discuss. When they call back, often you'll have moved on to a different activity. From the midst of the new activity your brain goes into overdrive, trying to recapture the point you'd planned to discuss. A brief diary note when it's uppermost in your mind will save that moment of anxiety and flurried recall.

Computer shortcuts ™

These tips are written from a Microsoft-user perspective, with extra tips for Mac users. It's not high-tech stuff so if you're a competent and highly trained keyboard operator, skip this section.

Key points

51   Keep the desktop of your computer clear of clutter — only display icons for the programs you use constantly, and arrange them to suit your needs.

52   Learn your keyboard shortcuts — you'll save heaps of time.

53   Back up all the time. A computer disaster is not an if, it's a when. Make sure you're not the one moaning about what you've lost.

54   Keep your hard drive clean and tidy. Use SCANDISK and DEFRAG regularly.

55   Use the Print preview facility to get a snapshot of the look and layout of your document.

56   Learn to use Windows Explorer.

57   Set yourself a goal to learn something new about your computer every week. Most people drive their Pentiums as if they were a 286.

58   Use templates — they save untold hours.

59   Improve your induction processes, and your ongoing staff training, so that everyone in the company uses intranet systems properly.

60   For web searches find a search engine you can understand, and use it to short-circuit your queries.

 Keep the desktop of your computer clear of clutter —
only display icons for the programs you use constantly,
and arrange them to suit your needs.

Usually, when a new program is loaded, it makes itself an iconic
shortcut that lands up on the desktop (that's the first screen you see
once your computer is open, for non-techno readers). Over time
your desktop starts looking like a multi-coloured, very crowded
domino board, and what used to be a shortcut becomes a daily
search to find the icon you need. In reality, you'll only use a handful of them regularly, and these are the ones that should be on the
screen. The rest of the programs are only a couple of clicks away,
accessed through your START, PROGRAM button.

To clean up the desktop (and if you're not sure, please don't do
anything drastic; check with your IT adviser first), hold the cursor
over the unnecessary icon. Right click with your mouse, and then
choose DELETE. You don't lose the program, only the icon.

You can also shift the icons around. I didn't know this until I
wanted to shift computer buttons off the screen saver photo of one
of my beautiful grandsons. Hold your mouse anywhere over the
screen, as long as it's not on an icon. Right click and some options
show up. Choose ARRANGE ICONS, and untick AUTO ARRANGE.

On a Mac you would simply drag the icons to your APPLE MENU
ITEMS folder, which lives in your system folder. This then creates a
pull down menu of all the programs (aliases).

 Learn your keyboard shortcuts — you'll save heaps of time

Here's a short list of some basic shortcuts you may find useful. (Touch typists who've been well taught, please skip this part, but pass it on to all your two-finger typo friends!)

Computer shortcuts:

➡ If you're in the middle of a line and wish to return to the start of the line, press HOME. For the end of the line, press END.

➡ If you want to go the beginning of a document, press CTRL (Control) + HOME at the same time.

➡ To get to the end of the document, CTRL + END.

➡ To highlight a word, hold the cursor over it and click twice instead of dragging the mouse along the word.

➡ To copy a piece of text, highlight it, and then hold down CTRL + C.

➡ To insert it move the mouse to the chosen spot, and then go CTRL + V.

➡ To cut and paste, CTRL + X and then CTRL + V, where you want it.

➡ To save, hold down CTRL + S.

➡ To shift the cursor along the line one word at a time, hold down CTRL + LEFT or RIGHT ARROW BUTTON.

➡ Once a word is highlighted you don't need to delete – just start typing. The highlight means it will delete as soon as the first letter is depressed.

➡ How to identify a shortcut. Any of your drop-down menus on the tool bar that have instructions on the right-hand side such as CTROL + ... are shortcuts.

For Mac users, simply substitute CTRL with APPLE (Command).

This is not a complete list. Take time to find more shortcuts. If you've got access to the *Dummies* books they usually have a selection of further shortcuts, and your other software programs will have their own special ones. (I love the *Dummies'* zany non-nerd language and humour). If this is new to you, you might like to copy this page and keep it by your computer until the strokes become second nature. Take a few minutes to let your fingers learn a neurological pathway to the shortcuts and you'll save hours of time over a year.

 Back up all the time. A computer disaster is not an if, it's a when. Make sure you're not the one moaning about what you've lost.

My computer friends tell me that about 80 percent of people take the whole situation far too lightly, and don't use a regular system to back up properly.

There are three levels of back up:

➡ Minute by minute, as you work on documents.

➡ To disk for anything really important, until it's completed and you've got a final copy, probably on paper.

➡ Regular and full back-ups of all your documents.

How often should you do a full back-up? The answer is, 'What can you afford to lose?' The frequency is up to you. You need to decide how much of your data you can afford to lose, should disaster strike. If you've just done a lot of new input, I'd suggest you should do it that day, even if it's not the normal back-up day. You can also do what are called incremental back-ups – just the new material each day, and a full back-up weekly. Get a computer specialist to help you set up these systems so you know everything is safe and the right material is being saved. Once installed, do a test run to make sure you are saving the right things. Learn how to retrieve the information should need ever arise.

Another safety precaution is to keep a constantly updated version of your work and key data away from your office. This is so that, if worst came to worst and you had a break-in or a fire,

if machines were stolen and your main back-up destroyed, your business could still run, your precious database would be preserved, and any other major project is also safe. Don't think some disaster won't happen to you – that's what they all say! I can't count the number of close business contacts who've had cause to share their own personal dramas!

Keep your hard drive clean and tidy — use SCANDISK and DEFRAG regularly.

Did you know that a computer needs regular housekeeping?

If you're a tidy person who's been trained in good computer techniques, this statement is so obvious you'll wonder why I bother to mention it. However, many computers long for a spring-clean. A computer that is not maintained is equivalent to a filthy, dirty house; dust under and over all the furniture, clutter left lying around for ages, things lost because they've been left in the wrong place, and dirty dishes in the sink.

Think of the regular internal maintenance of your hard drive as similar to the oil and grease you do on your car. If it's not done regularly your computer gets slower, the hard drive becomes inefficient, and you run the risk of your system crashing. To get rid of unnecessary temporary files or deleted material, start with DISC CLEANUP. Do the following two tasks when you don't need the computer for an hour or so. Close all programs, and every month run SCANDISK. Select THOROUGH and it checks your disc surface as well as your files and folders for errors. It will also fix them if requested.

The DISK DEFRAGMENTER is a clever process that goes through the whole system and rearranges everything tidily, getting rid of the empty 'holes' and leaving your computer faster and more efficient. Every time you turn off a computer without properly closing you chew up extra space inside. The path is START, PROGRAMS, ACCESSORIES, SYSTEM TOOLS. If you have trouble running either DEFRAG or SCANDISK, temporarily disengage the virus and screen-saver programmes.

55 Use the Print preview facility to get a snapshot of the look and layout of your document.

Most of us still like to see a hard copy of a document when we're proofing it. This is partly because it's very difficult to get an accurate view of the layout of the page when working on the screen. The answer for most people is to print off a hard copy, make the corrections, and then go back to the screen to do the final touches.

Printing out a hard copy is still the most popular way for most writers to get a sense of words and how they link and interconnect. However, if layout is the issue, it can very easily be done on screen.

On your tool bar (usually at the top of the screen) go FILE, PRINT PREVIEW and you'll get a small version of your document layout.

Play with the choices on offer. You can see one or more pages at a time, go smaller or bigger, magnify, and do heaps more cool things.

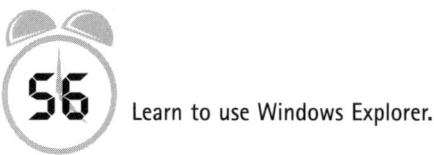

56 Learn to use Windows Explorer.

Learn to use Windows Explorer, it will save you hours of time. Windows Explorer doesn't look very sexy at first glance, but let me assure you, the tricks it can get up to are very delicious. With the flick of a wrist and the click of a key you've got enormous power over the innards of your programs. Files can be shifted in seconds from one section to another; your computer 'housekeeping' is made simple; the case of the disappearing file can be solved in a minute or two by using the FIND feature; and lots more. This discussion merely scrapes the surface.

The quickest way to open Windows Explorer is shift your cursor to the START button, usually on the bottom left corner of your screen, and right click your mouse. Choose EXPLORE, and your computer will obligingly open it. You'll find the entire contents of your operating system displayed.

If you put your regularly-used documents in MY DOCUMENTS, highlight that on the left-hand side and all your document folders will open down the right-hand side. As this is not a computer manual I won't go any further than to flag your attention to this wonderful tool. My strong suggestion is to get lessons from a savvy computer friend, or pay for training. This is definitely not an area to fool around in; you could do serious damage by experimenting without some guidance.

The FIND feature is another very cool detail. As with every computer function, there's more than one way to skin the cat. The quickest way to FIND in Microsoft is from the START button, or if you're already in Explorer, go TOOLS, FIND and you have choices of where to start looking. (In Mac it's simply APPLE + F.) If you really have no idea where you're going the machine will search right through everything, but it's a bit like giving someone the London phone book and saying, 'I want to find John L. Smith, and I don't know which suburb he lives in.' If instead you said, 'I'm looking for John L. Smith, who lives in Well Road, Hampstead', you'll get results much faster. The computer equivalent is to use the DATE and ADVANCED features to narrow the search.

Before we leave you to go exploring, let me give you one vital hint. I learnt it the hard way! If you want to move a file from one folder to another using Windows Explorer, COPY first. Once you've checked that it's safe in the new position, then delete the old one. Even though it seems very straightforward to shift files around, sometimes the machine gets indigestion. Just recently I shifted a very important Power Point document, with lots of extra data in the Notes section, to another folder (I was doing my housekeeping, keeping things tidy). To my utter shock and dismay, the Notes, which were an integral part of the document, vanished. The only way I could get them back was via my back-up. It took several conversations with computer boffins before I discovered that I should have copied first, and then deleted the redundant version from the old position (after I'd checked that everything was intact).

The newer Macs have a built-in HELP facility that features an extensive range of TIPS AND SHORTCUTS. With older models, visit www.apple.com and look for the same thing.

 Set yourself a goal to learn something new about your computer every week. Most people drive their Pentiums as if they were a 286.

Keyboard shortcuts, as we discussed in Key Point 52, are just the beginning. Computer productivity extends well beyond those few points. I guess it's because we're creatures of habit, but many computer users learn enough to get by on and then stop, unless forced to expand because of a new program or an upgrade.

Develop an enquiring mind. Watch what others do, and get them to explain. If you've got a fix-it person coming to do something to the mysterious innards of this hunk of metal on your desk, don't automatically go off and do something else. See what you can learn from them. (If it's very high-tech mechanical or electronic stuff I leave them to it, but when it involves programs and shortcuts, I always do a sticky beak. That's how I first learnt about Windows Explorer.)

What programs are you using only at a basic level? What programs don't you understand? Which is the most efficient way for you to learn? Although in some cases it might be to take a public seminar, I like to learn on my own computer. Even though it costs a higher hourly rate to get someone in, it is far more efficient.

You learn on your own machine, using your own programs (which may have been already modified slightly for your organisation), and you can ask questions specific to your machine. You learn at your own speed, and if the trainer is any good, they will tailor your programs for your own desktop efficiency. Also, you can usually ring them back with quick 'How do I ...?' questions. If they're any good they remember your machine, the way your programs are configured, and how to best explain something new to you – it's worth paying for this kind of support.

Another increasingly popular way to learn new programs is via on-line training. Many people like to access training they can practise in odd moments. (Our company is constantly evaluating the best of this kind of learning in order to provide extra value for our 'Getting a Grip on Time' web family. Check out the 'Links and Resources' section at http://www.gettingagripontime.com)

My final piece of advice on this point is to check out the skills of your own staff. Most people are willing to share their expertise, as long as it doesn't negatively impact on their regular work. Perhaps you could set up regular short training sessions, maybe even at lunchtime. Call it a 'Bag Lunch' and have fun. Find out what people want to learn. Share the training responsibility around; get everyone involved with questions and skill-sharing.

 Use templates — they save untold hours.

One of the most wonderful aspects of computers is the way they take routine tasks and shorten them. Every program you have in your machine will have the facility to create templates, which save you from typing repeated or basic information.

You can do it in your accounts package, your word processing package, your contact management system, your email or intranet program — in just about everything.

Let's look at a simple example. If your organisation uses a database or contact management system, you'll almost certainly have templates already with the software. Our company uses Act,

a fabulous product. We've got templates for our letterhead, faxes, invoicing, and a range of letters we send out on a regular basis. (The templates can very easily be modified when necessary.) If you were in our database and we wanted to send you a letter inviting you to attend one of our seminars, we would look up your name, and then choose WRITE, OTHER DOCUMENT. A range of templates we've already created would pop up in a little menu. One click on the chosen template and your full details are already on the page, as is the chosen letter. We can then alter anything we like, but the beauty of it is that much of the thinking and writing is already done.

One of my clients, a company in the health field with consultants who write lengthy reports on each patient, introduced templates. (Although the details for each report changed, the basic format didn't.) They found to their delight that individual report writing time reduced from approximately 1.25 hours to 45 minutes per report. Not surprisingly, they immediately experienced an increase of 30 percent gross turnover.

 Improve your induction processes, and your ongoing staff training, so that everyone in the company uses intranet systems properly.

Our company runs programmes for organisations big and small, in several countries. Not once yet (I'm waiting for the day!) have we found a company where everyone knows how to use their daily intranet communication tool efficiently.

So why not? you might well wonder. There are several different possibilities and variations on the theme, but the two basic ones are:

1. No one knows how to use it properly (and we've addressed that in Key Point 57).

2. The induction process and ongoing education system isn't good enough.

Typically, what happens when a new program is installed? Either the training or IT department runs group training for everyone. If you're lucky you get a good trainer and everyone reaches a good skill level.

If you're not lucky you get some cursory instruction and are left to sink or swim, bothering those around you for help if you get stuck. You learn enough to get by on, and no one, including yourself, realises that you're using only between five and fifty percent of the functionality of the program.

However, even if existing staff members fit into the first 'well-trained' category, someone leaves, or the company expands and new people arrive. They may well have never used your intranet program before. The assumption is made that they'll pick it up quickly — they probably think that themselves. If they're lucky they get a comprehensive explanation of the intranet. Problem is, everything is new, they're feeling overwhelmed, and at least 50 percent of what they're told in those first few days flies over their heads. So, what further training do they get? I can tell you, for we see the results. Typically, not much.

If they're unlucky, they don't get any help. Mention induction training in such companies and everyone gives a hollow laugh. The problem is we don't know what we don't know.

Let's take Outlook, one of the top-selling intranet programs, and give you one example. Most managers wrestle with how to keep tabs on tasks they've delegated. Even if they have Outlook, most don't know that it has a task allocation feature to assist tracking. Not only does the task request go to the delegatee, but you can set a reminder for yourself as well.

Internal email systems are one of our most powerful communication tools, and most people don't use them properly. How silly is that!?

For web searches find a search engine you can understand, and use it to short-circuit your queries.

My number one site for this purpose is http://www.askjeeves.com. I really like the way you can ask Jeeves an intelligent question, without having to do fancy tricks, stand on your head, and try and think like a tech-head. It is really an index of search engines, rather than a stand-alone search engine. And you're given a range of the most likely sounding sites in each search engine, based on the words you used, each with usually about ten one-line possibilities. This makes it very quick to scroll down the list and choose the one most likely to suit your needs. You've usually got at least 40 options on one page, unlike many regular search engines which deliver you possibilities in multiples of only ten.

Another good one is http://www.search.com, but don't take my word for it – go search yourself. There are always new and improved services coming online.

If you'd like more education on search engines, and a whole lot of other really useful and easy-to-follow education on the web, you can subscribe to the e-zine of my friend Gihan Perera at http://www.firststep.com.au. In this area, Gihan is one of the most highly skilled and helpful people I know.

*E*mail
management

Key points

61 Effective communication is not communication with everyone but only those who need it. Don't forget that a face-to-face conversation is often quicker.

62 Treat your INBOX like the top of your desk. Keep it empty of all but the current tasks.

63 Turn off the alert button — you get enough interruptions without encouraging them!

64 Don't go near your email while working on an important task — it will distract you.

65 Sign your emails using an electronic signature. It saves time, helps promote your business, and prevents frustration at the other end.

66 If you have a modern email program, you can block unwanted senders with a click of a key.

67 Develop good-practice rules, otherwise known as protocols.

68 If you're lucky enough to have a PA, get them to filter your mail.

69 Depending on your budget, there are several ways to access your emails from more than one computer.

70 It's just as important to clean out your email folders as it is the rest of your files.

 Effective communication is not communication with everyone but only those who need it. Don't forget that a face-to-face conversation is often quicker.

Everything has its light and dark side. Email is absolutely fabulous in the way it can communicate rapidly with people all over the world, but, for the same reason, it is absolutely terrible in the way it can reach people all over the world when it's inappropriate.

Also, because of its immediacy and virtually free access, we all need to take responsibility about using email as a communication enhancer, and not let it put up unnecessary barriers.

Be careful that people in your company don't use it as a means of avoiding face-to-face communication. There's a strong temptation for quiet, introverted people to hide behind their screens.

The CEO of a growing company noticed that before the partitions went up in their new office, everyone spoke face to face when they had a question of their colleagues. As soon as the chest-high partitions went up, the emails started flying to the people sitting next to them. She nipped it in the bud, and the frequency of internal email has been maintained at a sensible level, unlike many companies who have let the whole thing become a monster.

 Treat your INBOX like the top of your desk. Keep it empty of all but the current tasks.

I was running a programme for a group of senior managers in a housing company. The marketing manager said in despair, 'I'm so overwhelmed. I never seem to catch up, and my office is a mess.' She took me to see it, and she was right. It was a shambles. The seat of her chair was the only free surface in the whole room (and even that was often decorated, when colleagues wanted to make sure she'd notice things). I asked to see the intranet system they used, always a useful thing to know when you're conducting an internal programme. She flicked it open, and there before our eyes was an INBOX with 1519 messages in it. The poor woman had information overload everywhere!

I shared with her our methods of clearing up the paper war and strongly encouraged her to clear the clutter in the INBOX as well. The next week, excited, she reported a clean desk, an empty INBOX, and an enormously reduced level of stress and overload.

The secret is to use named folders and subfolders on the left-hand side of your INBOX, just as you would if you were using a metal filing cabinet. Once you've dealt with something, file it.

If it's important to keep both parts of the message together, and you've replied on the top of the incoming message, don't bother with filing the first one. Instead drag your reply into the folder. It gives you both pieces of correspondence.

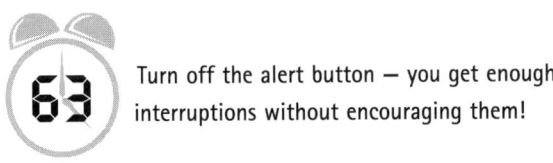

Turn off the alert button — you get enough interruptions without encouraging them!

The trouble is, most people don't have the self-discipline to stay focused on the task in hand when a little noise breaks their concentration, or a small screen imposes its cheeky self in their view. It's a bit like taking a peek at the mail. There might be a cheque, or a love letter, or news from overseas. Sure, but what's the main thing right now?

Instead, set regular reading times through the day. Most people find first thing in the day, if it's important to know what's come in, mid-morning, just before lunch or after lunch, and then later in the day are sufficient. If anyone has something really time-sensitive to tell you they shouldn't be sending it by email. A phone call or a fax is still the most immediate method of contacting each other.

To disable the alert you usually go through TOOLS or OPTIONS to turn the sound off.

 **Don't go near your email while working on an important task — it will distract you.**

I sometimes think I should start an Emailholics Anonymous club! I'm quite sure it's an addiction for some people, especially when we start to enjoy the benefits of exciting mail from faraway places or interesting people.

If I'm in writing mode I have to speak very sternly to myself to stay off the Internet until I've done my prescribed number of hours. Otherwise, those precious creative morning hours slip through my fingers like sand in an hourglass. Mail seems so demanding.

Here are some strategies to avoid addictive behaviour:

- Set yourself regular checking times, making sure they do not fall in your prime creative time.

- Have a clear view of what's important for the day. If you've got a big task needing concentration, don't go near your email until you've made a start. Check the mail as a treat and a light break.

- Set a time limit.

- First, have fun deleting as much of the crap as you can. Then, have a race with yourself to see how fast you can skim through the rest.

- Reward yourself for good behaviour!

- Every now and then, have a non-email day. It won't die from neglect. You might have a catch-up the next day, but you've given your brain a chance to detox. Very good for the health!

Sign your emails using an electronic signature. It saves time, helps promote your business, and prevents frustration at the other end.

We touched on shortcuts in Key Point 52. Your email (or digital) signature is another way of creating a shortcut. It's a pre-written signature. With a click you insert the words of your choice. (Most of these neat features are accessed through buttons like OPTIONS and TOOLS, but if in doubt check out your program's HELP menu for how to create a personalised signature.) You can have as many as you like, with the choice dependent on who you're writing to. Add your email address, postal address, phone and fax numbers, and URL (web address) if you've got one. It's like having a return address on the back of all mail leaving your company – it saves everybody time and prevents frustration at the other end.

Some companies use it as a little mini-promotion of something – it costs nothing, and as long as it's done with a degree of elegance, no one minds a bit of brief advertising. Just mind you don't go overboard!

And don't forget that some of your emails will end up overseas, so add the country and area codes to your phone and fax numbers, and include the country in your postal address.

If you have a modern email program, you can block unwanted senders with the click of a key.

Ever noticed that heavy-duty spammers lie? Junk mail plops into your box, you think 'this is garbage' and then, as you're about to hit the DELETE button you notice an address you can send back to for removal off their list. So, doing the right thing, you whack off a terse REMOVE note. Then, to your utter annoyance, you find yourself with a 'Sorry, we can't deliver this message' return back to your INBOX.

Most modern email programs give you the chance to block that sender. It doesn't stop all the others using sniffer dog techniques to hound you, but you have the small satisfaction of knowing that at least some of them will never muddy your waters again.

How? It will vary from program to program, but in Hotmail you have a BLOCK THIS SENDER option right beside the sender's email address. In Outlook 2000, it is ACTIONS, JUNK EMAIL, and ADD TO JUNK SENDERS LIST. For other programs, check your HELP menu. With Outlook Express you need to open the mail first. Then, a right click on the address gives you the option to block the sender.

Here's a *very* important point. Be very careful about opening attachments. Many viruses come as .exe files (and usually from trusted sources), innocently passing something on. Use a virus detector such as Norton and set it to scan all email and their attachments. Update your virus program at least monthly.

Develop good-practice rules, otherwise known as protocols.

I work with companies who use email at all levels. Some are just starting, and still enthusiastic about the benefits although you'll hear the occasional grumble when they get more than five emails in a day. Others are overloaded beyond reason – they pine for the days when they only got 50. These days they're more likely to get well over 100, and I've heard of some who get over 500 emails a day. Frankly, that's ridiculous.

In many cases the people suffering severe overload work for companies who don't have strongly enforced protocols (basically a computer term for good manners). Or their work requires them to be on a number of mailing lists, often known as groups.

Examples of basic protocols are:

➡ Don't copy your email to everyone, only to those who need it.

➡ Use REPLY, not REPLY ALL.

➡ Have one central person control group membership.

➡ Keep the groups up to date.

➡ If you don't wish to be on a group list, request the controller to take you off. You could delete it, but the problem will continue.

➡ Don't send unnecessary email, including jokes. Many people get annoyed by them.

➡ Don't pass on SEND TO YOUR ADDRESS BOOK type messages. Most of them are scams.

➡ Don't use email as an electronic form of 'cover my butt'.

➡ If you've got an issue with someone, don't get into a slanging match over the Internet.

➡ Private mail is not appropriate at work. Get your own Hotmail, and handle it at lunchtimes or after work.

The company intranet is not a free electronic version of the trading post, the local newspaper, or the notice board in the tearoom. Don't let people put in things like '1956 Holden for sale. One owner, top buy', or 'Charlie is going to the dentist. Don't call him for the rest of today, he won't be able to talk – ha ha.'

The people on Level 27 don't need to know that the printer on Level 20 is broken down. What about the invitation to cakes in the tearoom received by the Sydney office of a worldwide and very well-known IT company? Nice idea, but it would have taken them 21 hours to get to San Francisco! (Both true stories from my clients.)

There are heaps more possibilities, and the best way to develop them is internally. Have a brainstorm to see what's not working well, and look for solutions relevant to your organisation.

If you're lucky enough to have a PA, get them to filter your mail.

A well-trained secretary can reduce your load dramatically, in a variety of ways.

I believe that for at least another ten years we will continue to see managers who refuse to process email. (Not all of them are technophobic. Some just find it faster to process mail in paper form.) Some managers get their secretary to print off important mail, draft responses if that's appropriate, and they then only need to quickly cast their eye over the contents. This saves the manager drafting and typing, which often takes hours.

For those who do prefer to keep everything together in their computer, the secretary can be the first recipient, forwarding only what the boss needs to see.

If confidentiality between partners is an issue, or there are highly confidential client matters involved, a rule can be created using the tools relevant to your program. Look for tools named INBOX ASSISTANT, MAIL RULES, or something similar. You can set them to route mail wherever you choose, including a folder of your choice, instead of the INBOX where people are more likely to read things.

Depending on your budget, there are several ways to access your emails from more than one computer.

This tip is particularly useful for those who travel a lot or those who work at home some or all of the time and prefer not to have to transport a laptop back and forth from the company office (or your computer may not be portable).

High end

Ever been challenged by not having access to all your email correspondence, because you often work away from your desk? With a combination of Outlook (the full version, not Outlook Express) and Microsoft Exchange, this problem can be avoided. Provided your IT people can set up the appropriate Internet connection with your corporate network, it doesn't matter where you are in the world. If you have Outlook and Internet access you'll be able to collect your emails. Microsoft Exchange acts as a central place for storing emails. You're able to access archives, old messages, sent messages, folders, and attachments. Check out deals on offer (at time of writing the cost was between NZ$50–$200 per workstation). Microsoft has various licensing deals. There are other providers with similar and often cheaper products. Your final decision needs to take into account how well the chosen program functions, the value of the manager's time and the cost to the organisation when information can't be readily accessed.

The client who told me about this system now emails himself attachments of all his important files so he can access them from anywhere. It also solved the common capacity problem of too many emails stored on the company server.

Note: Outlook is much more than just an email programme. It can be used for scheduling, task management, delegation, and other organising functions.

Budget end

If you don't yet have the budget for Exchange and the value of your time isn't an issue for you, there's a free service – not as good, but it fills a gap. This function may not be available on all email programs. However, take a wander through your TOOLS options, find ACCOUNTS, MAIL RECEIVED, select your default mail program, select PROPERTIES, ADVANCED and, at least in Outlook Express and Outlook, you can select the option that leaves your mail on the server for any number of days you choose.

It's not as elegant as the 'higher end' product as you'll end up with doubled up email. If you want to keep answers on both computers, you'll have to copy to yourself in order to download them to the other machine.

It's just as important to clean out your email folders as it is the rest of your files.

In Key Point 62 we talked about using folders to keep your INBOX empty and control your email. Don't forget to prune or empty your folders from time to time, including your DELETED folder, just as you would a filing cabinet. It's one of those little tasks you can do whilst on hold for the Tax Department or the telephone company. Open a file, start at the oldest date, and select everything obviously obsolete. Otherwise your hard drive becomes clogged with a lot of junk.

If you're selecting mail scattered throughout the folder, hold down the CTRL button whilst you click on the relevant messages. Then delete them in a group. This still leaves the items not highlighted intact. However, if there's a block of messages you wish to discard, you don't need to click on each item separately. Highlight the top one, hold down the SHIFT key and then click on the bottom one of the group you've selected. This will highlight them all. Now you can delete.

Many larger organisations have an efficient archival email system that operates automatically, set up by the IT department. Test it from time to time to ensure that you really can retrieve any important 'stuff' you think you're keeping.

If anything is really important, use the SAVE AS feature to keep a copy in your word processing package. Then, no matter what happens to the old emails, you've got it. Another way to do this is by a simple COPY and PASTE, which takes a moment more but saves the untidy look of the web-based formatting in your word processing programme. This depends on whether you expect to

re-use the material, or whether you just want the information to look at.

If client information should be accessible to others in the company, save emailed client responses in a central source. Just having them on your own PC is poor information management and puts both you and the company at risk.

Paper-handling ™

Key points

71 If you haven't got the right equipment and storage facilities you'll never really control your paperwork, no matter how good your intentions.

72 The space closest to you is your most precious — make it work for you.

73 Store materials upright rather than flat.

74 Control your desk, or it will control you! Use drawers properly.

75 Be a decision-maker, not a procrastinator. If you can complete an action in two to three minutes, do it now. Don't defer what can more efficiently be done right now.

76 File, don't pile. Every time you stand up, put away the last batch of papers and equipment.

77 Your mother was right. Clean up your room.

78 Have you got enough years to read all the books you want to read? If not, either change your choices or learn to speed read.

79 Simplify and save time.

80 A place for everything and everything in its place.

 If you haven't got the right equipment and storage facilities you'll never really control your paperwork, no matter how good your intentions.

We need four critical areas to line up before we can be really productive at our desks:

➥ The right gear.

➥ Get rid of the clutter.

➥ Develop the right systems.

➥ Good discipline and habits to keep the systems flowing.

In my work, I see a wide variety of working environments ranging from pristine to disgusting. The habits of a very few incorrigible cases would be more suited to a pigsty. (In fact, pigs in their natural condition are very clean. It is humans who force them into smelly and dirty conditions.) However, most people do try.

Some have no idea where to start but a little bit of education can help fix their problems. Others have some work to do on their day-to-day disciplines. The ones I feel the most sorry for are those who clearly try but don't have enough storage. Often this situation is forced on them – the owners of the company haven't thought the matter through, or they've put money into the 'look' without thinking about the practicalities.

Start noticing how you can store and access your equipment and stationery supplies more efficiently. Improvements can often be made very cheaply:

➥ Perhaps you could add extra shelving close to your desk;

➡ don't forget the wall space around you, even partitions;

➡ empty airspace can often be better utilised;

➡ more streamlined furniture is constantly coming onto the market;

➡ your desk may have broken drawers or cupboards;

➡ check to see if you use the space under your desk efficiently (without toppling things on your bunions!).

The possibilities are endless.

The space closest to you is your most precious — make it work for you.

Take a step back and look carefully at your workstation. Is there anything within a hand's reach that you don't use regularly? Look into the cupboards and filing equipment nearby. Anything there you're constantly jumping up for? Monitor your actions for a week. How many times a day do you stand up to fetch something?

To some extent this is time and motion study. We're looking to minimise as many actions as possible. Anything you use at least once a day should live right at your fingertips, or at the very least only an arm's stretch away. Add up every unnecessary movement in a day and many people find they're wasting 15–30 minutes jumping up and down for things stored inefficiently.

What's on top of your desk? It took me years to work out that the cramped feeling when working on my desk was caused by the overabundance of tools and 'must have handy' items on the surface.

I've always known that you should have these things close at hand. However, the feeling of space and freedom once I put most of them in my top drawer surprised even me! Your top drawer may need a ruthless de-clutter first.

My top drawer now houses erasers, ruler, calculator, paper clips, stapler, sticky notes and a few other commonly used stationery items. Nothing else is allowed to lurk there. This means that you can always lay your hands on what you need at a second's notice, and the top of your desk is free for work.

The most important space is the V shape in front of you as you sit at your desk. What do your eyes constantly light on? Our attention span is short enough without placing distractions in front of ourselves. If at all possible, keep any 'pending' work out of sight, or slightly behind you. (See Key Point 74 for further ideas on how to store your work in progress.)

 **Store materials upright rather than flat.**

You've got a pile of files on your desk. Someone asks for one. You dig it out of the heap and pass it over, they quickly find what they need and give it back. Where do you put it? Back exactly where it came from? Not very likely, Charlie Brown! Unless you're a very exceptional human being (and fussy to boot) you'll put it back on top of the pile.

This might not matter in this case, especially if you're the only one normally handling your files. Problem is, your memory is constantly at work trying to remember where things are (and hopefully your memory has more important things to focus on). Plus, the next time you want something out of that pile, especially if it's one you haven't touched lately, you find yourself spending a minute or two thumbing through all the files: a golden chance to be distracted.

The solution is blindingly obvious, but again not as common as it should be. Stand everything upright, or suspend materials in filing equipment of some sort.

Let's start with books (I'm not an ex-librarian for nothing, you know!). If you place them upright on a shelf, alphabetically by author's surname, not only will you quickly become familiar with their lodging place, but others will be able to go straight to the shelf if you're not there. Even more importantly for long-term order, a gap is created: it becomes very simple to put the book back where it came from.

You may have other placement systems. One of my associates places everything of one colour together – he's wired for colour, not words. Others position by subject, but sometimes a book covers more than one subject. The least changeable and variable factor is the author's name.

Miscellaneous soft-cover papers, magazines or catalogues have special needs. Most loose paper will go in a filing cabinet, but sometimes a topic is too large, or the items too bulky. Use upright periodicals boxes. Coloured manila folders create subsets. The contents are quick to see, retrieve and return. You can also very swiftly identify and discard anything obsolete.

Depending on the shelves used, archival boxes of paperwork can often be treated the same. Avoid the 'flat to stack' system. Instead, 'stand to grab'.

What about your day-to-day working files? In Key Point 74 we'll talk about how to use the filing drawer in your desk. However, if you suffer anxiety attacks when your important work is out of sight, don't panic now, we've got another solution. Get a stepped file or some alternative on your desk return (I fondly call them toast-racks – not their official name).

The key point is that every file is held upright and you can see, reach and return each folder to the spot it came from, with the stretch of a hand.

Control your desk, or it will control you! Use drawers properly.

I get paid to be nosey, so see the innards of more desk drawers than most people. Guess what? About 80 percent of folk don't use their drawers efficiently. Typical contents range from old files they're 'going' to sort out; their purse (sometimes that's because they're not given any secure place to keep their personal possessions – very bad office design); a few tatty ancient files they've forgotten about; their running gear; courier tickets (hidden so no one else pinches them); and chocolate biscuits (also hidden). The list is long.

As I approach a person's workstation it's very easy to know what we'll see when they open their drawers. The clues are strewn all over the top of their workspace. Stacked, spread, layered and untidy pregnant piles of 'stuff'. The ingredients of the drawers vary but the look doesn't. The impact is always the same – inefficiency and poorly handled paperwork.

Our drawers are designed to support *us*, not the mice planning their next move. So, what should be there? you may well ask. The numbers of drawers in a desk vary, so use the following suggestions as a guide.

➡ If you've got only one top drawer and a file drawer that holds suspension files, you're in luck. You've got a very efficient layout. Put your tools in the small top drawer and hang your current project and action files in suspension files in the big one. Key point: in the file drawer, label every file and place them in strict alphabetical order. Include the following named categories:

ACTION/CURRENT: for your current paperwork. (If you diary-note when you need to start each task you can safely put them out of sight without forgetting them.)

ACTION/PENDING: for the things you're still kidding yourself you might get to! Not of high urgency, but would be nice to get to if you can. Usually no deadline.

➡ Any current project files that will be more useful at your fingertips. All labelled.

➡ Halfway to the Rubbish Bin (File 13 or the Round File – let your labelling imagination run wild!). The importance of this file far outweighs the value of the items snuggled up in its loving arms. Here you put the 'I don't think I need this, but I'd better hang on to it for a while' paperwork that would otherwise take up over 50 percent of your desk space, let alone your head space.

➡ Small drawers but no file drawer? Allocate one drawer for current action files and one for the Halfway to File 13 stuff. The small space forces you to keep your clutter pruned.

➡ More drawers? Lucky you. You'll have room for personal things, frequently used stationery, scrap paper and scribble pads, your choice of CDs to play in your computer, your business cards and similar goodies. Monitor yourself; watch for small things you use constantly; and if possible keep them in your drawers, NOT on top of your desk.

 Be a decision-maker, not a procrastinator. If you can complete an action in two to three minutes, do it now. Don't defer what can more efficiently be done right now.

After speaking to a group of credit managers, one man came up to share with me his best time strategy. He is known in his workplace as an excellent time manager.

'I have a very busy and responsible job, with many people coming to me every day for help with things,' he said. 'I noticed that other people didn't seem to get through as much work as me, so I started to observe what I did differently. What I realised is that most people leave things lying around, thinking they'll get back to them. I've learnt to finish a task as it arrives. Sometimes the next person has to wait a moment whilst I complete something, but long-term it saves bucket-loads of time. You don't have to refamiliarise yourself with an item you've already put some time into. It's done, and your mind is free to get on to the next task.'

Develop a compulsion for closure. This is one compulsion that I encourage. (The dark side is perfectionism, and if you're suffering from that, in your heart of hearts you'll know!)

File, don't pile. Every time you stand up, put away the last batch of papers and equipment.

Ever seen a large untidy heap of papers and been told that's 'the filing'? Ever wrestled with the tedium of having to 'do' the filing? Ever felt challenged about keeping your environment tidy?

Raising six very busy little children taught me this key point. I had to find a way to streamline, or I would have gone mental tidying up after them all day (or the house would have been a permanent disaster). If you do it frequently enough, but not too often, filing and tidying up becomes a very quick and almost invisible process.

The business application is as follows:

➡ When you finish a task put the completed materials either on the furthest away point of your desk, out of your immediate visual range, or even better (as long as it doesn't cause a traffic jam), on the floor beside or behind your chair. Which side of the chair they go on depends on which side of the room their final destination lies.

➡ The next time you stand up, instead of stepping over the seeming clutter on the floor you ALWAYS bend down, pick it up, and put it away.

Although it seems an untidy way of working, in fact it is very efficient.

Even though there is a slight delay, you're still putting things away while they're fresh in your mind. It's rarely longer than 30–60 minutes before you're putting away your current crop of 'stuff'. You never end up with an intimidating pile of filing (and I've seen some beauties over the years). Over a year many hours are saved. You walk around less. If it's filing you don't need to refamiliarise yourself with the item or paper in hand, and it hasn't interrupted your flow of activity.

The bottom line is it saves you from two possibilities: either spending ridiculous amounts of time being tidy, or living in a permanent state of chaos.

 **Your mother was right. Clean up your room.**

Perhaps it's because our mothers told us to do it that so many seemingly well-organised, highly paid and otherwise neatly-turned-out adults ignore this sage piece of advice!

Funny thing is, the same philosophy applies at the highest level of business, and most really successful people are rigorous in their application.

> Kerry Packer, the richest man in Australia and head of a media empire worth A$3000 million, used to regularly do a tour of inspection with his PA, after most of the workers had left for the day. The first time an employee went home leaving their desk messy, a warning. The second time, dismissal! (No doubt some employers wish they could still operate this way.)
>
> Add people like mystery and suspense writer Jeffrey Archer; Richard Branson, whose companies include the Megastore retail chain, Virgin Atlantic Airlines and V2 Records; industrialist and author Sir John Harvey-Jones, former chairman of ICI — all three are meticulous about keeping paper under control. Surely it makes sense to listen to successful people.

How many desks do you see covered with dead trees and miscellaneous equipment? How many drawers and cupboards hide a fascinating selection of junk? How many factories and workshops have areas with an embarrassing mess of lurking clutter? What's the archival storage room like? (How about your home garage?)

And what's the energy level and productivity of the people who work in this mess day by day?

Have a 'clean up the office and workshop' day. Everyone with responsibility for the 'stuff' to be sorted comes to work in old clothes. You might like to order pizza in for lunch, have plenty of rubbish sacks, and make it fun. Dedicate the day to clearing out the clutter and throwing away anything obsolete. Sort out all equipment so it's easy to find and label if necessary. Prune the filing cabinet, clear the paperwork off desks, return everything to its proper place, and label shelves, boxes and files. If you don't have someone with a logical and systematic way of handling paperwork and setting up easy systems, bring in an outsider to help you. (We have Clutter Busters in our organisation, and know many more. Drop us a line if you're stuck – we may know someone nearby.)

If you clearly need more storage and shelving equipment, purchase it before the clean-out. However, if the clean-out could possibly create more space, save further purchases until later. If you buy beforehand you may find you don't need what you've bought.

 Have you got enough years to read all the books you want to read? If not, either change your choices or learn to speed read.

In the deluge of information most people drown under, look at exactly what you spend your time reading. Do you read as much as you'd like, or as many as you'd like of the books you're interested in? Have you ever ploughed through a book purely because you felt you should finish it, rather than because you were enjoying it?

I was fortunate enough to do a speed reading course with Dr John Demartini (http://www.drdemartini.com). You might like to ask yourself the same questions he asked of us:

➼ How many books do you read, on average, in a month?

➼ Multiply that figure by twelve.

➼ How many years of life would you like to think you have left?

➼ Multiply the number of years by the number of books you can read in a year.

➼ That figure is the likely number of books you'll read in the rest of your life, unless you learn to read faster.

How do you feel about that? Faced with that knowledge, are you happy with the selections you're currently making? The time spent on today's reading prevents you reading something else. Life is one of choice so make sure your choices take you in the direction you wish to go.

Find a rapid reading course (sometimes called speed reading) in your community. We have an increasing list of recommendations on our website (http://www.gettingagripontime.com). You'll also find some pointers on speed reading, but please don't consider this the definitive instruction. It's much easier and more effective to learn in a classroom.

Once your mind has been stretched to learn the techniques, the most important element is their ongoing practice. You've been reading in a certain way for most of your life, and that style isn't going to shift permanently after a few hours of training. You are the most important ingredient in your success (sorry, there isn't a magic answer and one-stop solution!).

Another way to have more reading time is to cancel subscriptions to papers and magazines you don't have time to read. Get realistic.

 Simplify and save time.

How many companies and individuals do you know who try to make things complicated? The problem is, our conscious mind blocks out after only a few chunks of information, no matter how clever we are.

Some clever mathematician has worked out that, at any one time, we're bombarded by two million bits of information. At a subconscious level, we chunk them down to about 134 manageable pieces, which are then further filtered by our brain. At a conscious level, however, we can handle only between five and nine separate items simultaneously. If you've ever asked the way to somewhere and been given long, involved directions, you'll know what we're talking about.

We suffer unnecessary complexity in every walk of life, including the unwieldy forms you fill in for banks, insurance companies and airport landing cards. (At the time of writing Fiji has one of the worst I've ever had to fill in – a ridiculous repetition of information and a very poorly designed form.) Add internal workflow processes, instructions for staff and even some complex diary systems. The list goes ever on.

Every year run an audit on yourself and your company. What can be done better and more efficiently? What forms are poorly designed? What processes are not now necessary? What regular things are we doing that could be performed more efficiently?

I ran a six-week time management programme with a rapidly expanding and very successful international security firm. One junior member of staff wanted help on how to reduce the pressure of a routine data-collection and report-creation task, run by the company since Adam was a cowboy. Fortunately we had a very senior staff member in the room. When he heard the question he looked at her in shock. 'Are we still doing that?' he said. So we dug a bit deeper. The quality of the question determines the quality of the answer. Suddenly, a whole new raft of questions needed to be asked.

'Why are we collecting this data? Where does it go? Who uses the information? It may have been useful when we were a small company, but does this process still need to be done in the same way? Even if we continue part of the process, what shortcuts can we take?'

Within five minutes, a whole new way of looking at the problem was created. The process was obsolete, and the staff member was freed up to use her time far more productively.

 **80** A place for everything and everything in its place.

I was speaking at a conference and took the opportunity to sit in and listen to another speaker, a very funny senior academic from one of Australia's universities (not your normal combination – I bet his students have fun). As an aside he had a moan about how he was always losing things.

> 'I drag my weary tail in from work, dump briefcase and keys in the first empty spot I find, and head to the fridge for a beer. Then next morning I rush round madly looking for my keys, blaming the wife and kids for having shifted them.'
>
> Quick as a flash from the back of the room came, 'Put them in the fridge.'
>
> The room erupted.

The point, however, is exactly right. If you've got only one place to put things you won't waste time and energy trying to remember unnecessary details. This is where a system pays off.

You might be thinking, 'Robyn, you've just told us in Key Point 79 to keep things simple. Does this equate?' Absolutely. Very simple systems and processes require probably as much thinking as complex ones to set up. They also require a bit of self-discipline to get into the habit. However, once your subconscious has developed a neurological or cellular memory (alias a habit), it requires no further effort and your wonderful brain can spend energy on things that make a difference.

*M*eetings™

Key points

81 Before you accept an invitation to a meeting, ask yourself, 'Do I need to be there?'

82 Send the agenda with the invitation.

83 At the beginning of the meeting, re-establish the agenda and the finish time. It keeps everyone on task and focused.

84 You can be on time for meetings! Block out fifteen minutes either side as soon as you accept.

85 Don't wait for latecomers. Start without them or leave, even when it's the boss.

86 Send any relevant printed material before the meeting, preferably with the agenda.

87 Don't allow phones in the room.

88 Don't let a meeting go more than an hour without a break. People's attention span is dictated by what happens in the lower part of their anatomy.

89 Make minutes useful. Use short, punchy action points and have them distributed as soon as the meeting is over.

90 The chairperson's key role is control: it's not a privileged soapbox.

Before you accept an invitation to a meeting, ask yourself, 'Do I need to be there?'

Meetings are held for all manner of reasons. Don't automatically accept an invitation. Ask some questions first.

> One of my regular coaching clients (we'll call him Peter), a senior partner in a very large multinational accountancy firm, was overwhelmed with staff meetings, team meetings, training and coaching meetings with his people, partner meetings, client meetings, professional development meetings, other peoples' departmental meetings when they wanted input from other sections of the firm, 'nice to have you along' meetings, and any other 'let's have a meeting for the sake of a meeting' kind of gathering that could be dreamed up. (And in a firm of thousands, that's easy!)
>
> There were other factors as well, but the issue of meetings was having a serious impact on Peter's departmental productivity. His team couldn't access him enough, he wasn't there to drive the direction of the unit, younger staff were struggling, and he constantly worked ridiculous hours to try and keep up with the real work. This impacted on his family, his health and his well-being.

We came up with a series of simple questions to use every time he received these irresistible invitations (and if you're a nice and obliging person it's often very hard to turn them down). Some of them you may not ask directly, but have them as an overlay to your acceptance or rejection of the summons.

➥ What is the purpose of the meeting?

➥ Is it related to my overall goals?

➥ What do you expect from me?

➥ How long will it last?

➥ For which part of the agenda will you need my input?

➥ I may need to leave after my contribution. What time will you be dealing with the topics related to me?

➥ Do I really need to be there?

➥ If you need input from our department, can someone else attend instead of me?

➥ Are decisions likely to be made that only I can make, or can I delegate or sidestep?

Using these questions, Peter was immediately able to reduce his attendance. He even turned down meetings with other partners that he formerly would have automatically accepted. The result was less stress, more productivity and profitability, and happier staff.

82 Send the agenda with the invitation.

This gives you a couple of major benefits. If it's a work meeting it enables people to make a better decision about whether to accept. It also flags the items that will be under discussion, so that you can arrive prepared. This is especially important if something might be contentious, or if the item can't progress without researched input.

Are you often invited to meetings that, had you known the topic, you would not have attended? Here's a radical suggestion. Don't go unless you receive an agenda at least 24 hours before the meeting. However, don't deny them the pleasure of your company unless you've given the organiser notice that this is now a key requirement for your acceptance. Courtesy first, firmness second.

At the beginning of the meeting, re-establish the agenda and the finish time. It keeps everyone on task and focused.

Some years ago, I had the good fortune to work on a large training project with a very efficient woman. Helen was a wonderful role model on how to run good meetings. She was the project manager of all the training for a Telecom New Zealand subsidiary, and liaised with clients, providers and the staff of her own company. I was the time management specialist her training company had chosen to work with. She started every meeting with great courtesy and great control (and this applied whether there were ten attendees or two).

'Thanks for coming. This meeting will finish by ...'

In a group meeting she kept control by then saying something like, 'The items I have for discussion are ...', and she would very quickly read them off the agenda she'd already circulated. 'Does anyone have other topics they'd like to add to the list?'

If it was a meeting with just the two of us, she started with, 'Great to catch up again, Robyn. Before we start, let's do a time and agenda check. What time do you have to be gone by?' It was a great focusing question and kept us very task-oriented.

Once that was handled, she would then do me the courtesy of saying, 'Now, what items would you like covered?' After receiving my contributions she added her own. Very rarely would she allow us to digress off the agenda, tempting as it can be for people who've become friends. Extraneous conversation was put aside until the end of the meeting — if we had time.

You can be on time for meetings! Block out fifteen minutes either side as soon as you accept.

Ever noticed that most big companies have an insidious culture of running late for meetings? It almost seems that the bigger the organisation the worse the problem.

Of course there can be a number of contributing reasons, but one big one is very simple and ragingly obvious: people don't allow themselves enough time to get there.

If you work in any organisation bigger than about four or five people all in the same room, you'll have walking time, quite aside from all the other factors. Add a few floors, slow elevators, or even different buildings to travel to and from, and no one is surprised when people run late. Then, insidiously, it becomes the norm to start late and run over time. I don't believe it's ever acceptable (unless there are very unusual circumstances).

Trouble is, there's not only the travel time. What about toilet time, 'gather my wits' time, the quick and urgent phone call, the last-minute 'please help' from a staff member as you head out the door, the coffee and water time when you get to the other end? It's as if most people go into a time warp and blank out reality. If even one prompt person is waiting, the company resources and money are being wasted. Try doing a cost analysis on that in any decent-sized company and you'll be horrified at the price tag.

Here's another way to deal with this issue. Whether you're using a paper-based diary, a LAN (local area network), or a combination of the two, the same solution applies. As soon as you accept an invitation to a meeting, block out the travel time and fifteen minutes either side of it.

If you manage your own diary and no one else sees it, this will act as a prompt when you're tempted to slide in 'just one more thing'.

If you share your schedule via your internal LAN, others can electronically search to find the gaps. As soon as they find one, whoosh, you'll have a meeting to accept or reject. Then you don't like to muck others around, especially if you know it's hard to find gaps when everyone is free. So, set it up beforehand. You then control your schedule instead of being controlled by everyone else.

In case any reader thinks I'm setting myself up as a paragon of virtue, in my early years I perfected 'being late for meetings' so well that one boss kicked me out with, 'Don't you ever come late for my meetings. Get out, I don't want you here!' Thank you, Jeremy. It was a great lesson!

 Don't wait for latecomers. Start without them or leave, even when it's the boss.

'That's radical,' you might be thinking. Sure, but I've seen it done with great effect. Obviously all things need to be considered, but let's look at what we're saying here.

Take the big picture position. Who's constantly late? What impact does it have on the productivity of the others, the efficiency of the meeting, and the culture of the group? (Every group, even a voluntary one, has a culture.)

Perhaps my perspective is a little coloured from raising six kids, but if you don't train people to your expectations you get what you deserve. The chronological age and seniority has nothing to do with it.

Let's look at some possible ways to deal with the tardy ones.

⇒ Suppose you're an on-time chairperson and one of your people is regularly late. You could treat them as Jeremy did me (see the previous Key Point). It wasn't the first time I'd been late.

⇒ Don't go over things they've missed. It's their responsibility to catch up, and unfair to the prompt people who have to listen to a recap.

⇒ Some make the late person take the minutes.

⇒ You might hassle them in a fun way.

⇒ Some companies have a fines system, or the late one has to shout beers on Friday or chocolate cake for morning tea.

What if the person who called the meeting is constantly late? It

may be appropriate to start without them. The other alternative is to leave. Even if it's the boss, give them five or ten minutes' grace, then go back to your work. You may choose to leave a note: 'Decided not to wait – we knew you wouldn't want us wasting our time!' or some other appropriate comment. Be diplomatic, use humour, and make a stand.

However, be cautious of career-limiting moves! At present you may feel this wouldn't work; perhaps your boss is a very dominant person who expects obedience. The interesting thing I've noticed with such people is, a staff member who stands up for what they believe is almost always treated with respect by the senior person. If you're unlucky enough to work for a boss who doesn't show their staff respect, are you in the right organisation?

 **Send any relevant printed material before the meeting, preferably with the agenda.**

During a programme for a firm of lawyers one of the team (not a partner) came up to me in the break.

> 'Robyn, would you please talk about the appropriateness of bringing lots of reading matter to a meeting and expecting your colleagues to read it on the spot.' Obviously I asked a few questions to find out the reason for the request. His senior partner, who ran the meetings, was the guilty party. At nearly every meeting he'd arrive with lots of paper, pass it out to them, and then expect them to skim-read and be able to discuss the points he wanted to cover.

How good are you at doing two things at the same time, when both require full concentration? It's a rare human being who can do it.

The cost to the firm of a group of experienced and highly paid lawyers sitting around a board table reading materials is alarming, especially if they're your lawyers! They should have been given the chance to peruse and think about the information before the meeting.

87 Don't allow phones in the room.

A very large international IT company asked for a course on 'How to run effective meetings'. It was the weirdest session I've ever run: a brilliant example of how *not* to run meetings. The trouble was, the CEO had a different work ethic to the rest of the company. She'd been sent to Australia from the States to do the job, and had no family in the country. Her work was her life, and she expected her managers to behave in the same way.

The session was a bun fight! People came and went like yoyos, phones rang constantly, and although everyone had chosen to come, the activities of a number of the group were so (unintentionally) disruptive that it minimised the learning of the rest.

Half the people were late, several sent messages to say they didn't have time to come, and many of them insisted that they had to leave their mobiles on because they were not allowed to be

out of communication range at any time. When questioned, the same applied to holidays and weekends. Their CEO's belief was that their job demanded 100 percent availability. Bluntly, that's rubbish, except in exceptional circumstances.

And there was more. Even though they'd scheduled the training weeks before, one fellow informed me, very embarrassed and apologetic, that he had to leave halfway through. He'd been ordered that morning to attend a last-minute meeting and no excuses were accepted.

Many of this company's problems could be solved only at a higher level, but there was something those folk could have done to minimise interruptions.

If at all possible, find a back-up person to take your calls when in a meeting. It may be a PA. In a genuine crisis they know where to find you. Then, the meeting isn't interrupted with the miscellany of calls many people field in a day.

If you find yourself running a meeting where phones keep going, ask people why they need to be on. Depending on your seniority, either encourage or request they be turned off.

Another option, if there's no external resource to take your calls and it's absolutely critical to be contactable, is to turn the ringer off. If your key contacts are programmed into the memory, the tiny sound the 'silent' phone makes will draw your eyes. You then have the option of choosing to leave the room. However, most calls will be able to go to the message bank.

Don't let a meeting go more than an hour without a break. People's attention span is dictated by what happens in the lower part of their anatomy.

If our bladder is full, our bottom numb or legs need a stretch, our ability to concentrate is almost non-existent. If a meeting must go longer than an hour, give everyone a few minutes' 'stretch and stand' break every hour or so. However, be clear about how long they've got and get started immediately when people come back into the room.

The other benefit is that our brains have had a chance to refocus. Long, unbroken marathons of brain gymnastics are not efficient. In any activity (not just meetings) a short break for a coffee or a stretch gives the subconscious a chance to process and access other information. You'll be far more effective when you return to the task in hand.

Make minutes useful. Use short, punchy action points and have them distributed as soon as the meeting is over.

Some people make a meal out of fancy and elaborate minutes. This is not the place to major in perfectionism (unless you're a parliamentary or court recorder). Keep them short. The simplest type of minutes can be done using a template similar to the one below. Keep a copy of the template in your word processor and run it off before each meeting. All you usually need are action points and a record of who's doing what. If there are regular items on the agenda that need quick discussion, they can be pre-written on the sheet.

And one more point. How useful are minutes that come out the day before the next meeting? If they're distributed within 24 hours of the meeting it will save confusion over who is doing what and be far more likely to bring results.

Template for minutes

Date:			
Attendees:			
Purpose:			
Item	Action	By whom	By when

The chairperson's key role is control: it's not a privileged soapbox.

How many poorly run meetings have you attended? Ever noticed a chairperson who uses their position to grandstand and bulldoze their own agenda, leaving battered and silenced colleagues grumbling into their teacups in the corridor. I'm sure some people believe that's their right as a chairperson, especially when they're the boss. However, there are infinitely more effective ways to build co-operation. Domination is neither a good team morale strategy nor an effective use of people's brains!

Let's check out how an effective chair handles the group:

➡ Functions: the agenda; control and atmosphere of the meeting; 'the buck stops here'; making sure that everyone contributes; ensuring that the tasks are evenly shared out, and that willing horses don't end up with all the work (conditional on individuals' time constraints, of course); impartiality.

➡ If you need training, get it. An effective chairperson can make or break the effectiveness of any meeting.

➡ Be structured. Don't dodge all around the agenda. Stay focused on one issue at a time, finish, and then move on.

➡ Give trivia the time it deserves. If something is urgent but relatively unimportant, put a time limit on discussion.

➡ Watch the quiet people, and involve them. It is very easy for these folk to be dominated and talked over. Just because they are quieter and not in such a hurry to air their opinions doesn't mean that they don't have very valid things to say.

➥ Ensure that the vocal members don't dominate the meeting. If someone wanders, a chairperson has to kindly but firmly thank the garrulous one, saying something like, 'Let's hear from ...', or 'I think we need to keep on the topic.'

➥ Side conversations. These can be huge time-wasters and the chairperson must nip them in the bud immediately or the precedent will be set. They may have to stop the meeting and INSIST on only one person speaking at a time. If the pattern has already been set in an existing group, put it at the top of your next agenda for discussion. Once you've got consensus about not allowing side chat, the rest of the group will usually help the chairperson enforce it. The minute-taker can also assist by saying, 'I think we're off the point. Is this to be minuted?' Anyone who wants to chat socially can carry on after the meeting.

*M*anaging
the
home-based
office

Key points

91 Manage the interruptions or they'll manage you.

92 Use phone divert. It gives you a life.

93 Schedule written appointments at the beginning of the week with yourself, in your diary, for regular uninterrupted time.

94 Get a mentor, coach or support group – it's lonely out there. You need objectivity, support and people with positive expectations of your success.

95 Don't try and be perfect at everything – it's impossible. Hire consultants to do the bits you either don't like or don't do very well.

96 Pay for good training and technical support when it comes to your computer.

97 As quickly as you can afford it, delegate. Your business won't grow until you do.

98 You're not married to your business, even if sometimes it feels like it. A small amount of planning saves large amounts of family stress.

99 Get savvy about online resources – look for ways to do more with less.

100 Create contextual markers to separate home and work.

Manage the interruptions or they'll manage you.

As the Internet dramatically changes the way we communicate, around the world an increasing number of people choose to reverse the trend of the last 200 years. They gladly go back to the way their ancestors worked, running their livelihood from home. We all know about the many benefits and savings, including travel time, office overheads and reduced interruptions from colleagues. However, there are some unique challenges, and one of them is the different type of interruptions.

Have you ever woken up bright and sharp, the work at your desk beckons invitingly, you can't wait to get started, and then the day turns to sh...muck? One thing after another claims your attention, the rest of the world is clearly in a conspiracy against your productivity, and at the end of the day you collapse into an untidy heap of exhausted humanity.

You thought you'd escaped from this nonsense by waving a glad goodbye to the corporate world? Well, the interruptions are different, but you're not! It still comes back to self-discipline and useful strategies. If you can't control your interruptions you'd best go back to commuting for an hour each way and let other people tell you when to work, when to play, and how to run your day.

92 Use phone divert. It gives you a life.

If you can't bear not to answer the phone, try diverting it to a pager service or serviced office if you need uninterrupted time for important high-concentration tasks. Usually you can ring in for messages, get faxed lists, receive them on a pager (and your mobile may be able to double as a pager), or be notified by email. The other benefit is that you create the impression of a regular office when a real person answers the phone.

Unless you've got a mini-switchboard or Commander-type system in your home, most telephone services these days have message services that do the job of an answerphone. If you've got this feature you usually have a number of programming options, including instant diversion without a ring in your office.

Another huge benefit is that you can set the calls to follow you by diverting your landline to your mobile. These days you can run your business from anywhere (including the golf club, the hairdresser, or the beach).

However, a word of caution. Don't forget to turn the phone off as well. The world won't stop if you're not available for a few hours. If you've done your customer service right your clients won't abandon you, and even new prospects will generally leave their contact details. You didn't go into self-employment to still be married to the phone and other people's demands (or if you did, take a good look at yourself). If you're on holiday for a week, leave a message to tell people when you'll be back. They'll appreciate the opportunity to make alternative temporary arrangements if it's urgent, and you'll have a peaceful and well-deserved break.

93 Schedule written appointments at the beginning of the week with yourself, in your diary, for regular uninterrupted time.

This is an expansion of Key Point 5. Plan your week at the beginning of the week, and allocate times for yourself, by yourself, to do planning, development, long-term projects, or even office admin time. You won't grow your business unless you learn to be very self-disciplined about this non-contact time.

There's something about a written appointment. It gives you more power to say, 'No, I'm sorry, I can't stop for a cuppa or a chat' to Auntie Susie who was passing by or a family member who wants you to run an errand.

On the other hand, if you're sitting at your office through the wall from the kitchen with an empty diary, it's very easy to be sidetracked into thinking, 'There's no appointments on today so I can spare some time for ...' (whichever alluring time-stealer that's bobbed up).

There's another application. It helps you identify those who are supportive of your goals and those who really don't care.

Until 1987 most of my life was spent in rural areas or provincial towns, where the pace of life is very different from the major cities I've since lived in. I'd been in Auckland for about five years, had just started my own training business, operating from home just as most beginning service businesses do, when I got a call from a country acquaintance.

'Hi Robyn, we're in town for the next few days, and would love to come over and visit.'

'Great,' I said. 'It'll be lovely to see you. Hang on, I'll check the diary.' The last thing I wanted Karly to do was waste a journey across town through busy traffic and find me not at home, or with a client.

There was a silence at the other end, and then a rather miffed voice said, 'At our place people are welcome to drop in any time. We don't expect our friends to make appointments.'

I was stunned. She would never have expected to walk into commercial premises and have me drop everything. And then I realised that this woman had no idea of:

1. how to run an effective business,

2. didn't appreciate that I was saving her time by making sure I was there when she arrived,

3. didn't care that I may have needed to schedule her around other important activities, and

4. had no interest in my goals and efforts to establish my business.

Don't waste emotional energy worrying about such people – they filter themselves.

94 Get a mentor, coach or support group — it's lonely out there. You need objectivity, support and people with positive expectations of your success.

In your Small Office Home Office (SOHO) business, do you sometimes find yourself overwhelmed with major concerns, and unable to see the wood for the trees? When we work alone, or without peers to bounce ideas off, it's very easy to lose objectivity.

In a traditional work environment, you can use others as a sounding board, a benchmark, sometimes even a prick in the side to keep you moving. In your home office environment you rarely have that luxury. Your nearest and dearest may be your greatest fans, believe every word of your most optimistic publicity, but lack the experience to help you through your dark times.

Or, you might find yourself in a wilderness, with little support from your loved ones. Many self-employed people spend the first few years of low income and hard relentless work with bewildered family saying, 'Why don't you get a real job?' In your darkest moments you look at your corporate friends with their regular incomes, expense accounts, company cars, paid holidays and weekends and evenings away from the office, and wonder the same.

Try one or more of the following suggestions:

➡ Join a network of other SOHO operators. They're springing up in most areas.

➡ Find other business networking groups that give you the support you need. They may be within your industry, but don't need to be. The most important factor is an atmosphere of support and encouragement.

➡ Surround yourself with real friends who believe in you before you believe in yourself. Until you experience this, you can have no idea how powerful a gift they give you.

➡ Pay for a mentor or coach, and use them (at least) monthly. They don't need to know a lot about your industry; their most important skills are objectivity and facilitation. In fact, their questions about why you do things the way you do can be very powerful.

➡ Join or start a mastermind group of like-minded and supportive peers.

Mastermind groups are a very powerful springboard – they help to escalate your progress. An ideal group is anything from three to seven. Most meet once a fortnight for an hour or two (depending on the numbers). A typical agenda is a quick share of the latest news in each person's business, and then either one or two of you under the spotlight; or a timed focus on each person talking about either a set topic or a topic of their choice.

Don't try and be perfect at everything — it's impossible. Hire consultants to do the bits you either don't like or don't do very well.

Where do your skills lie? Find good contractors to fill in the gaps.

In the early years of my business, when still a one-woman operation, I struggled to do my own books for the accountant. One year I foolishly let one of my clerical staff have a go, sucked into hoping her assessment of her skills was correct. But she didn't really know what she was doing. As a consequence, for yet another year I was late with my returns, even though I spent hours pouring over figures.

The whole field was an endless struggle. I had only a vague understanding of the complexities of taxation requirements. As with most start-up companies, the major reason for even attempting this thankless task was a desire to keep the costs down. The problem is, while you're going ten rounds in the ring with calculators, bank statements and ledgers of endless columns of figures, you're not out there making the money.

Big lesson: hire experience. Any core area of your business is not worth skimping on.

Pay for good training and technical support when it comes to your computer.

This is another of those areas small businesses often try and save money on. Pay for good software trainers when you install new software.

> Our company uses Act, an exceptionally good and inexpensive contact management and database system. I cringe when I calculate the money and time wasted in our first two years of Act ownership. We mucked around for hours with the manual, trying to work out how to do basic things — which fields to use, how to do labels and mail merges, and even the correct way to enter data. As for using templates, applying the program's power to marketing initiatives, and a myriad of other exciting functions it offers, we were babes in the wood, with absolutely no idea! I thought I couldn't afford the training; instead I wasted my time, my staff's hours (all with a dollar value), and business opportunities.

The same thinking applies to all aspects of your technical and electronic equipment. Bite the bullet, find external contractors you can understand and trust, and pay for their time, advice and assistance. You still have to take responsibility for the results, but let the experts teach and guide you. One caution — don't believe the first person that says they can do what you want. Get referrals from people who've already used them, give them a small job to see whether you can get on together, and take an intelligent interest in what they're doing.

Wherever possible I try and learn something from my external providers each time they come into my office. I don't want to do their work, but if I understand more of what they're doing I can be more intelligent in my requests and trouble-shoot my own minor problems. As staff change (as they inevitably do), the intellectual property I've paid for hasn't all walked out the door. I'm able to at least point the new person in the right direction, even if they need a little bit of professional coaching.

As quickly as you can afford it, delegate. Your business won't grow until you do.

If you've got the desire to build a big business, if you see yourself as a budding entrepreneur, and you've never read *The E-myth* by Michael Gerber, rush out and get it immediately.

One of the key points Gerber makes is that being self-employed is not the same as being a business owner. If you're good at what you do and decide, based on that skill, to go into your own business, all you've done is buy yourself a job. A business owner, on the other hand, isn't wedded to the service or product that's provided. They see themselves as separate from what the company does, and if they've done their job well the company can not only operate quite well without them but is also an entity that can be sold.

Not sure what you can delegate? Don't know if you can afford it? Try writing down a list of all the regular tasks you do in a week and estimate the amount of time spent on each activity. Now, pretend you're paying someone a wage relative to each task and put a dollar value beside each item based on the guesstimated hours spent. For example, bookkeeping might be worth $35 per hour. If you've spent two hours this week doing the books you'd put $70 beside that one. If, on the other hand, you've done data entry, that may be worth $15 per hour. You've taken 30 minutes, so $7.50 goes in the column.

Ask yourself, 'What is my hourly rate when I'm engaged in income-generating work? If I were able to free up some of these other tasks, would I be able to do more of my work, and if so, what income could I generate?'

If it's higher than the value of the miscellany of tasks you've spent your days ploughing through, you're doing the wrong work, and you're underpaying yourself. Find a part-timer or contractor until you can afford to pay more wages, and keep your focus on your work.

Every start-up business goes through this soul-searching. The need almost always comes before we have the money to pay for help, but if we don't take that step we'll never have the money to pay anyone, including ourselves!

You're not married to your business, even if sometimes it feels like it. A small amount of planning saves large amounts of family stress.

Perhaps you left your corporate job or set up a partial tele-commute connection at home because you thought you'd enjoy a better quality of life and have more time with your loved ones. Now it seems that every waking minute is being consumed by work.

You can still have the quality of life you desire, if you plan for it. However, it takes serious commitment.

My friend Peter Miller, one of Australia's top corporate compères and professional MCs, shared this idea.

> 'My daily deadline is 3.15 p.m., when I stop work to pick up my kids from school. It's then our time together until about 8 p.m., by which time my wife is home and we've had dinner as a family (unless I'm doing a job, of course). Once they're in bed I often work until 10 p.m. in my home office.'

These suggestions come from Bronwynne Bandiera, of Brisbane, Australia. She says:

> 'I always plan at least two outings or projects for the weekend, and I'm ruthless with my commitment to them — nothing stops them going ahead. It could be watching the netball on Saturday afternoon, rollerblading for two hours with my kids, a picnic, a visit, whatever, as long as it means I'm doing something I love to do.
>
> 'In addition, a "time tip". I always take an hour out on the weekend with a cuppa to plan the menu and the shopping list for

the coming week. This takes the, "What are we having for dinner?" drama out of each evening. It also ensures that I have everything I need on hand to cook each meal.

'I also look at what's happening that week, what kids need to be at where, when and with what. All information is pasted on the fridge, the idea being, for example, "Okay, it's Monday. This is what's for dinner. If you're home first — go to it!"'

Get savvy about online resources — look for ways to do more with less.

More and more resources to streamline business, no matter what size or where it's located, are becoming available online. We won't get very specific in this book, for the speed of change on the Web would limit the usefulness of this tip, but use your favourite search engine to check under 'Home Based Business' or 'Home Office' and see what resources are listed. Don't forget to ask others as well.

We posed some time-saver questions to our 'Top Time Tips' subscribers, and from Lyn Garrett in Auckland, New Zealand, came this great suggestion.

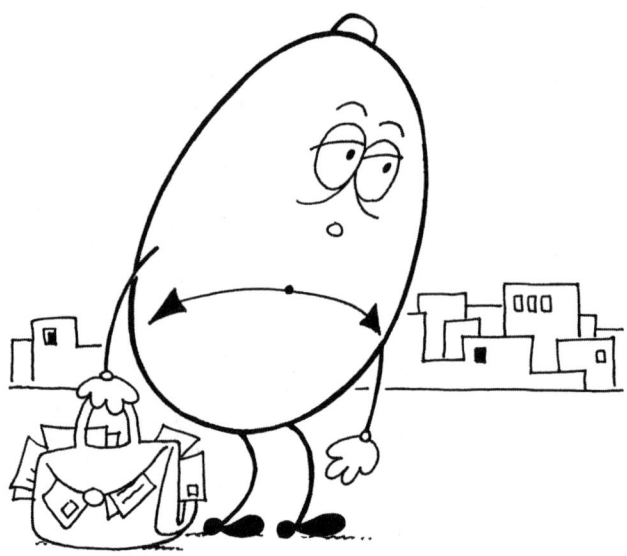

'The best time-saving tip I have is using on-line banking. My salary is direct credited to my bank and from home (often on a Sunday) I can pay all my bills from my computer. I can select which bill to pay, how much to pay, which day to pay it, and transfer amounts between accounts. No more standing in queues, writing out cheques, leaving envelopes in my bag for days before stopping at a post box!

'And I can also check that my tenants have made their automatic rental payments.'

After following Lyn's advice and setting up my Internet banking access (only a short phone call was needed), I was delighted to access my Australian bank accounts from an Internet café in Edinburgh, Scotland. Different countries and different banks will have a variety of resources available, but the key point is to constantly check out what's available. Service and functionality improve day by day.

The Web provides us with a myriad of wonderful services to save time in a world where we're all aiming to do more with less.

 **Create contextual markers to separate home and work.**

Phillipa Challis, another speaker mate from Victoria, Australia, uses this strategy.

> 'Six months ago I moved the business from a CBD address to a purpose-built office 30 steps from the back door of our residential address.
>
> 'I now find it easy to separate home from work. When I pick up my handbag and keys and take them into the office I am at work. I can move between the office and the house but until I take the bag and keys back into the house I'm focused on work. At all times I am dressed "professionally" to receive clients.'

Others have similar but different strategies, such as walking out the door in their business clothes, and then back in again, or driving around the block. The key thing you're looking for is a contextual marker, a way of signalling to your brain that now you're in work mode. It could even be as simple as turning the computer off or on, or shutting your office door.

Travel time ™

Key points

101 Be ruthlessly minimal in your packing — pretend you're a backpacker!

102 Carry any vital documents or items in your carry-on luggage.

103 Use luggage that saves both your time and your back.

104 If you travel a lot, or work from home extensively, use your laptop as your main computer.

105 Use travelling time in the way that's most productive for you right then. Rest or work? You decide.

106 A few days before you head off into the wild blue yonder, start a 'destination pile'. It makes packing even faster.

107 Sort and temporarily file as much as you can as you travel. This makes unpacking back at the office much faster.

108 While you're away, get your assistant to streamline and prioritise incoming mail and be your ears and eyes.

109 If cost is a factor when retrieving your emails or making phone calls, try to avoid the hotel systems — you'll need to take out a mortgage to pay the bill!

110 For the latest information on travelling technology, track developments on the Web.

 **101** Be ruthlessly minimal in your packing — pretend you're a backpacker!

Experienced travellers know this one, but it is still tempting. You look at that new tie or suit, the extra pair of shoes, the spare jacket you may need if it gets cold, and you add it to the pile. Bad idea. You waste time packing and unpacking at the beginning and end of the journey, at any new locations, and you clutter up your hotel room with unnecessary gear; you risk damaging your back heaving heavy bags off and on luggage carousels, and what if the bag was lost?

This is not the time to trot out your latest and best, unless it's a gala occasion and you're the celebrity guest. Use conservative and versatile dark clothes that can be used for more than one occasion. If you may need an overcoat it can double as a dressing gown. Socks will do instead of slippers (although you don't need them at most hotels). When you've selected your clothes, stand back and say to yourself, 'What can I do without?'

There are a few things for your comfort that are more important to pack than the extra clothes. I always carry my Swiss Army knife and a small pencil-torch. (I can't begin to count the number of times I've needed the knife. The torch? My Girl Guide habits die hard.) I also take my preferred coffee — some hotel coffee is crap — and if I'm rooming with someone (as you sometimes do at conferences) I take one of the eye-patches they give you on long-haul overnight plane flights. If you can cut out the light you generally sleep much more soundly. If you sleep well you'll be efficient the next day.

A huge time-saver is to create a checklist on your computer, and tick it off as you pack. Have a personal one, a business one, and a list of optional extras. I find I can now pack for an extended overseas trip in about 30 minutes. As long as you've got your clothes clean and ironed and in the wardrobe, they take only a minute or two to throw in a bag.

 Carry any vital documents or items in your carry-on luggage.

As you pack, ask yourself, 'What must I absolutely have with me tomorrow?' Whatever it is, take it in hand luggage.

Many experienced professional speakers tell horror stories of arriving in airports with their overheads, client notes and even their suit for the presentation in a few hours' time nicely packed in the bag that's gone to China.

If you can't be flexible, be prepared for the worst. One of my friends had a very important meeting in another city, starting at 7 a.m., and needed his secretary with him. When they arrived at 10 p.m. the night before, her bags had gone on vacation. She is a very immaculate and particular young woman, and the loss of her gear devastated her. Apart from all the drama and delay at the airport and then the hotel, she was so inflexible that it was beyond her wildest nightmare to appear at the meeting the next morning in what she'd been wearing the day before, and with no make-up. She refused to attend, and Gordon had to do the meeting without her. What a waste of time and money!

Here's a bonus tip. A couple of other really good things to carry onto the plane are a bottle of water and a snack if you're doing the long overnight hauls, especially long, cross-zone links like the one between Australia or New Zealand and America. I'll give the airlines the benefit of the doubt and assume they're trying to get you into the eating patterns of the destination, but you get quite hungry. Water is important because, even though they provide water, you get dehydrated. Your own bottle enables you to sip when you feel like it, not when it's convenient for the crew.

 **Use luggage that saves both your time and your back.**

I love people-watching in airports. You can tell at a hundred yards who travels a lot. Their baggage tells the story. A new corporate traveller has round shoulders, an exhausted face, and arms almost touching the ground. They're weighed down with a bulging-at-the-seams briefcase on one side and a useful but heavy computer bag hanging off the other shoulder. If they've come international, they've also bought their duty free goods before they got on the plane. Definitely a modern-day version of a camel.

On the other hand, ever watched what the airline crews carry off a plane? Copy them.

Forget heavy briefcases and computer bags. Go buy yourself a cabin-size wheelie or trolley bag instead, and make sure its handle pulls up at a touch. In goes your computer, spare battery if it's a long flight and you plan to work, your bottle of water, eye-patch for sleeping, work or reading for the plane, the client file for the next day, your travel and hotel documentation, and essential personal items to get you into the next day, should the worst happen.

Your trolley bag isn't quite as elegant as a standard briefcase when it comes to business meetings, but you can still use it as a briefcase. People don't even raise an eyebrow – they're smart and functional. If you really don't want to use your wheelie for business, pack a smart folder or soft satchel.

Add to this a suit bag over your shoulder instead of a big suitcase, and if you're on a short trip you may even be able to carry everything onto the plane, saving time at check-in and the luggage carousel.

 **If you travel a lot, or work from home extensively, use your laptop as your main computer.**

One of the biggest hassles when travelling is if you don't have your regular information at your fingertips – it's back in the computer on your desk. Using network cables, it's a reasonably simple and inexpensive process to regularly synchronise your files between laptop and desk machine (if you don't know how to do this, get help from your IT consultant or department).

However, the big issue is email. Surely one day the Big Boys will get programs synchronising better, but at present it's not so easy for Road Warriors to transfer all their emails to their laptops, and vice versa. We talked about some other strategies in Key Point 69, but if you really move around a lot and use Internet access in the various places you find yourself, it's much more efficient to do everything on the laptop, including when you're back at the ranch. Then you're never without any key information, things are dealt with as they arise, you don't have to call the office or ring the client back, and you're ready to get onto new tasks on your return.

One important detail: get a big screen and keyboard for when you're in the office. They can easily be plugged into the extension on your laptop, which gives you better working conditions.

For goodness' sake don't waste time with those horrible little internal mouse things – I hate them! Always carry a mouse and mouse pad. I even use my external mouse in the cramped conditions on a plane. (It's amazing how you can juggle the peanuts and the wine glass!) One caution: plug the mouse in before you turn on your laptop: it doesn't like new things added after it's talking to you.

You may be saying (especially if you're not a touch typist), 'Robyn, the internal mouse is fine. I can use it easily.' Good for you, but beware Repetitive Strain Injury, for your hand is cramped while you use it. Also, I'll guarantee you're slower on your computer than anyone of comparable speed with an external mouse.

Use travelling time in the way that's most productive for you right then. Rest or work? You decide.

Isn't it fascinating to watch people get on their soapboxes. Trouble is, they often forget that others have different needs and priorities.

In the last few weeks I've picked up several articles about business travel, and to my amusement the various authors have taken completely opposite table-thumping positions about what you should do while you travel.

One school says, 'Don't waste your time watching movies or reading light novels while you travel. It's productive time you're frittering away. Take your work and maximise your time.' On the other side you hear, 'Don't be one of these Type A people who feels they have to work every minute of the day, who can't wait for the plane to be airborne so they can pull out their latest wizzbang computer and start work. Take a good book and enjoy the opportunity to unwind.'

For my money, it depends what you need at the time. Both are right, but neither is completely right, for there is no one way. Let your intuition guide you as to the best way to use your time. I always go prepared to work, and if I've got a tight deadline on something I treat travel time as pure gold – if it's air travel there are no interruptions from phone, email, clients or staff.

One of my friends gets a lot of business from chats on planes and in airport lounges. Although I'm a very friendly soul and an enthusiastic networker, for me travel time is my time, and I prefer not to engage in conversation. Every time Christine tells me about her latest 'connection' I question myself, but I choose not to worry about possible lost business opportunities. Be comfortable with your own style.

You'll find, if you expect it, that much of your best thinking happens while you travel (and that includes train, boat, bus and car). Never go anywhere without a pen and notebook – as soon as you haven't got them you'll want to jot a great idea down.

What about recreation? On a long journey I always tote a novel. If the mood takes you, there's nothing more delicious than a few hours to bury yourself in a good read. It switches off that busy brain, relaxes your whole body, and you arrive refreshed.

 A few days before you head off into the wild blue yonder, start a 'destination pile'. It makes packing even faster.

I learnt this one from my good mate Matt Church, one of Australia's top speakers, and a consummate professional. I used to share office space with Matt, and one day I noticed several 'untidy' piles around the floor. When I looked a bit closer I saw little stickers with 'Hong Kong', 'Citibank', and 'TAB'. They were jobs he had coming up.

> 'Robbie, it makes it so much quicker when you're getting ready. As soon as I think of the first thing I want to take to a job, I start a pile. Any time you think of something you'll need to take, just add it.'

I've been doing it ever since. (My piles are neatly on a side table, Matt). Another thing that happens is that every time your eye lights on that growing little heap your subconscious thinks, 'Now what else has to go.' Most times you're not even aware of the process, but by the time the day to pack rolls around you'll find most of your requirements are just waiting to go in the bag.

Sort and temporarily file as much as you can as you travel. This makes unpacking back at the office much faster.

I used to get tired looking at the big pile of miscellaneous 'stuff' that poured out of the bag every time I got back from a trip. Now I pack a few coloured plastic A4 envelopes. Each night, back at my hotel, I sort out the clutter for the day and file it. One is for receipts, another for data entry, a third for filing, and a fourth for Action (basically, anything else that requires some work by me). You could have another one for your assistant, if you have one.

 While you're away, get your assistant to streamline and prioritise incoming mail and be your ears and eyes.

If you have an assistant, get them to identify the mail into priorities (No. 1, 2, 3 and so on) as they open the mail for you. On your return, instead of having to work through a depressingly high pile (all the while thinking, 'Why do I bother to go? There's always so much to attend to on my return!') you can immediately get straight to the most important tasks.

Even if it's another day or two before you're up to the lower-priority piles, at least you've got the confidence of knowing the most important tasks have been handled, no clients are going to disappear, the suppliers are not about to go on strike, and the bills are handled.

If you're away for more than a day or two, and really do need to know what's going on back at base, have a simple daily Activity Report sheet drawn up. Basically all it needs to record is a summary of activities, phone calls and mail, what the requests were, what's been done and by whom, and what action is next required. If items have been processed and put away, it may be helpful to know where they've been filed or stored. Have it either emailed at the end of each day if you have easy Internet access, or faxed ahead to your hotel.

 If cost is a factor when retrieving your emails or making phone calls, try to avoid the hotel systems — you'll need to take out a mortgage to pay the bill!

Phone calls can be economically handled by using a calling card. It may be one you've organised before you left home. Even a pre-paid phone card of the country you're in is almost always one of the cheaper options. Be careful about using your credit card in a phone box. Even though it seems nice and easy, sometimes there are extra charges and minimum call rates. You could find yourself with an expensive bill and very little to show for it.

If you choose to forward your email to a free Web service, you'll be looking for Internet cafés.

Having done a month's travel in the US and around the British Isles, and paid sometimes very large amounts of money for Internet café access, it was a treat to come across the easyEverything Internet café chain. They are in a number of major city locations including Edinburgh, London, New York and a number of European locations.

For £1 you get a varying amount of time, depending on the demand when you first log in, but often that pound buys you an hour or more of access. Each café has over 400 computers, great coffee, a good range of food, excellent service, and 24-hour access. It made keeping in touch with the office a pleasure. More information about their service is at http://www.easyEverything.com.

 For the latest information on travelling technology, track developments on the Web.

I recently stumbled across http://www.laptoptravel.com — a really useful site. Not only does it sell goodies to make laptops more useful, but there are some really useful articles. For instance, here is a summary of how to access mail when you're travelling internationally.

International ISPs

Don't assume you have to ditch your current online service in order to connect overseas. The major Internet Service Providers (ISPs) maintain local access numbers around the world so you can go online by placing a local call. Get these numbers and check out the cost of the service and how it works before you leave home — generally available online or by calling the ISP's 0800 number (or 1800 for Australia).

As a general rule, the bigger the service provider, the better its international network.

Plan ahead. ISPs' offerings vary extensively in convenience and price, so finding the right solution at a reasonable price can entail substantial research.

For one option, check out http://www.ipass.com, and there are others.

*B*alancing
work
and
family

^{TM}

Key points

111 Get the priorities right. The search for balance between work and family is the cry of our times.

112 Choose to work for organisations that support flexibility.

113 Balance doesn't come automatically: we have to plan for it. However, sometimes balance is neither possible nor desirable. A perfectly balanced life all the time would probably be rather boring!

114 When you're happy at home you're happy at work.

115 Every six weeks have a flexible weekend, being as free and slothful as you wish. NO work. If possible, extend it to three or four days.

116 Block out family and holiday time at the beginning of the year.

117 Make housework almost invisible (apart from the serious cleaning). Put things away as you go.

118 Involve the rest of the family in the chores and family responsibilities, including financial, if that's appropriate.

119 Hire a cleaner, and any other assistance you need.

120 Look for streamlined ways to help you keep the household chores under control.

 **Get the priorities right. The search for balance between work and family is the cry of our times.**

More and more people are starting to question the frenetic pace they seem to be sucked into in their daily lives. You can't get home in time to see your children before they go to bed? You haven't got time to take a lunch break? No chance to exercise? Wrong thinking.

A senior executive and father of a young family was shocked to hear his three-year-old son refer to him as the 'Breakfast Man'. He stopped to consider what this meant, and realised that the only time Damien saw him was at breakfast. His habit of very long hours had not changed after his children were born, his wife accepted his beliefs that some things couldn't be changed, and so life had continued in much the same pattern post-children as before they came into his life. His little boy's words caused a dramatic shift in his thinking.

It was surprisingly easy, once he was clear on his values and priorities, to reorganise his hours and spend more time with his family.

 **112** Choose to work for organisations that support flexibility.

I came across the next contributor through the book she co-wrote with Susan Biggs. It really gave me hope that some companies are starting to think about this whole issue in a more creative and proactive way. Even though many of the examples in the book are Australian, the message is relevant in every country.

Kerry Fallon Horgan, author of *Time On, Time Out! Flexible Work Solutions to Keep Your Life in Balance* (Allen & Unwin), has the following to say.

'Men and women of all ages want greater balance in their lives. In an international survey of more than 1200 business students from 30 universities in ten countries, overwhelmingly what the students wanted was to have a balanced lifestyle and a rewarding life outside work. The increasing trend toward employees seeking work and personal life balance has also been found in organisational surveys where the majority of people surveyed would choose increased flexibility even at the cost of career advancement and would turn down a promotion if it meant spending less time with their families.

'Progressive organisations are acting on the knowledge that their people are the key to success. These workplaces realise the huge financial benefits. They enjoy improved morale and performance, increased commitment, staff retention, decreased absenteeism, stress reduction and competitive recruiting.

'I could give you many examples, but let's just take one. The AMP Adviser Technology Helpdesk team has been working

effectively from home for the past four years. Each person works a week at home then a week in the office. That team has reported a 20 percent increase in productivity, and no one has resigned since they started this practice. This kind of work usually tends to have about an eighteen-month turnaround.'

You can find out much more about Kerry's work at:
http://www.flexibility.com.au.

 Balance doesn't come automatically: we have to plan for it. However, sometimes balance is neither possible nor desirable. A perfectly balanced life all the time would probably be rather boring!

My belief is that when we are in start-up mode on pretty much anything it is near impossible to be balanced perfectly in all areas of life. If balance is our overriding principle, we run the risk of never creating enough momentum to get our desired project(s) off the ground.

Think of a jet plane. Consider the fuel and force required to get that huge weight into the air. However, once the plane reaches cruising altitude and levels off, the amount of fuel, energy and focus required is less. So it is with learning new skills and commencing new businesses. Ask any successful person whether they

initially had a period of time that was way out of balance. I believe that early imbalance is an integral part of success, and then it becomes critical to seek life balance again.

However, the price of ignoring balance for too long is profound. I've done it myself in earlier years — it's what got me into this whole topic of time management. I got tired of being tired all the time, of feeling driven, of feeling I always had to complete everything, achieve every goal, be superwoman, supermum, superlover, perfect at everything. It was too hard.

Stories abound of highly successful people in every arena, so focused on their big goal that they went beyond breaking point and suffered a traumatic reversal. They may have been running a business, building a high-level career, making buckets of money, winning a sporting achievement, or developing skills in a particular area. And then something cracked. The reversal is sometimes financial, sometimes health, and in many cases it is relationship-based. There was nothing wrong with their focus, except they kept it going too long. They kept the plane rising when it was time to throttle back.

We can be out of balance for a short time, but it's critical to our long-term success so we need to recalibrate and re-evaluate once in a while.

114 When you're happy at home you're happy at work.

Let's give the illustration of this key point to one of my 'Top Time Tips' subscribers (see our website to register). Michael Rabey is a real estate agent and auctioneer for L.J. Hooker in Canberra, Australia.

> 'Robyn, I am sending this to you on "Nicholas Thursday". That's the day I spend with my eleven-month-old grandson. Doing this allows my daughter to reduce to two days the need to place Nicholas in daycare. The real truth is that Nicholas and I have a ball every Thursday. When he's sleeping I work, when he is awake we play. The clients who know what I do think it's great; those that wouldn't think it great, don't know. Mobile phones work very well from home, and I take control of my schedule by not making appointments on Thursdays.
>
> 'By the way my sales have increased this past six months compared to the previous six months. Andrew Mathews, who was another of the speakers with you at the L.J. Hooker Convention at Royal Pines, said, "When you are happier at home, you are happier at work. When you are happier at work you are happier at home!"'

Everything is connected.

 Every six weeks have a flexible weekend, being as free and slothful as you wish. NO work. If possible, extend it to three or four days.

The temptation is, when you're learning a new job or carrying a very heavy schedule, to just keep going. After all, there are the evenings and weekends, aren't there?

However, and probably just as well, our bodies were never designed to keep going non-stop. Think of your body like a rubber band. If it's at stretch all the time it will snap much more quickly than if it's given time to release pressure.

It was explained to me another way by a nutritionist.

'It all relates to stress', she said. 'If you think of all the stressors in your life as individual stress bricks, every time you experience a stressful situation, or are particularly busy, you're building a stress wall around yourself. If you just keep going the wall has nowhere to go but up. The people who live this way push themselves all year, take a holiday, and spend the first week being exhausted and usually sick.

'The best way to keep the stress wall at a healthy level — enough to keep you vibrant and alive, but not so much that you're overwhelmed and ill because of it — is to take a break of a few days every six weeks. This knocks some of the bricks down and keeps the wall always at a manageable height.'

A school adviser shared with me the plight of a young first-year teacher. She was building stress walls big-time! It had reached the middle of the year; she was working late every night, coming in on weekends, and always struggling to keep ahead of the work. When he questioned her, she'd had no free weekends since the beginning of the year. This is what he recommended:

> 'Every four to six weeks, leave school at the same time as the children on the Friday afternoon. Don't come in on the weekend, don't take any work home, and forget about work for the whole weekend. Arrive back on Monday morning in time for the staff meeting, not before. If you don't start doing this, you'll burn out, and the education system will have lost another bright keen young teacher.'

She took his advice immediately, and her teaching skills and ability to handle the work improved dramatically.

 **116** Block out family and holiday time at the beginning of the year.

Ever noticed that if you leave things like holidays or time off for when you 'have time', they don't seem to materialise? If you haven't got your holidays planned yet for the next twelve months, get out your yearly planner and do it right now!

It is quite amazing how everything comes together when you set a strong goal to do something. Often you'll first be tested as to the degree of your commitment, and then it seems a magic wand is waved – things just seem to click into place.

This point applies not just to big chunks of time, but also to 'time out' on a regular basis, for the activities or people you really want to be with. In Key Point 114, Michael has achieved it with his little grandson. What wonderful joyful moments are you denying yourself, purely because you haven't put enough thought and planning into it?

Take a minute to consider the following questions.

⟹ What one activity would you love to spend more regular time on? Is it golf, sailing, bush walking, time with kids or loved ones, reading, studying a new interest ...?

⟹ So, what stops you?

⟹ And what one thing would you need to do in order to change the status quo? Why don't you give it a go?

You might be surprised how things can be moved around to fit your intentions for a more balanced life.

 Make housework almost invisible (apart from the serious cleaning). Put things away as you go.

There are so many time-saving tips for housework it could be a whole book, but let's throw a few quick keys into this pot-pourri of ideas. People who have tidy houses, skip over this page. You know it instinctively. If, however, you're still aiming for perfection, there might be one or two ideas here to help.

In case you haven't noticed, the people with tidy homes (as well as offices), seem to arrive at this amazing state without any obvious effort. Most of them don't appear to spend huge hours every week rushing busily around with a vacuum and duster. In fact they seem to have more free time than their messy brethren. You won't find them with three days of dishes in the sink, an overflowing basket of washing, and a littered house. How do they do it?

I didn't start out life very tidy, I must confess, but over the years I've learnt the trick to never having a messy house is to develop a compulsion to closure, to finish what you start, and put things away as you go.

Organised people never wait for a task to get too big before they attend to it:

➡ Do a load of washing every few days — don't save it to the weekend. If you put it in the machine as soon as there's enough for a load you'll never have a disgusting laundry to deal with.

➡ If you're in an apartment or flat you might use a clothes horse to dry your washing. One load fits easily. If you use a dryer, fold the clothes immediately — it saves most of the ironing.

➡ If you've only got a few dishes, rinse them under the tap as soon as you've finished, dry and put them away. It's very quick, and the clean sink makes you feel good.

➡ Hang your clothes back in the wardrobe as soon as you take them off, or at the very latest the next morning, before you put clean ones on.

➡ Have precooked meals in the freezer for the nights you're too tired to think, let alone cook.

➡ And here's a radical thought (it kept me sane in the busy child-rearing years, and I've lived by it since): don't be a perfectionist. Be tidy but not fussy. Dust is not mould. So there are dust curls under the beds? Who's looking? Will it matter in five years' time? Have fun, and don't take life too seriously.

Involve the rest of the family in the chores and family responsibilities, including financial, if that's appropriate.

Thank goodness the days of believing that women are the 'owners' of the domestic duties have started to go out the window! Make family members responsible for their own mess, right from a very young age. Put children on a household duty roster, including cooking duties. Even a five-year-old can prepare vegetables and plan a simple meal.

What about adult children? Anne Rennie, best-selling Australian fiction author, shares these great ideas for harmony in the house.

As most offspring nowadays live at home until they are in their late twenties or early thirties, once they're earning even a modest wage, negotiate them into installing a second phone line, complete with handset and answering machine. The initial cost is small, the time-saving and reduced friction enormous.

All their incoming and outgoing calls come to this new number and can be diverted to their mobile. In the initial stages, instead of handing over your phone to your offspring, give the caller the new number and politely explain the new arrangements. Do not answer their phone! Your offspring have complete control and responsibility for their phone, including paying the bills. They can talk for as long and as often as they like on the phone. You have a phone line available 24 hours a day, you no longer have to worry about escalating phone bills or waste valuable time and energy arguing to be allowed to use your line, or answering calls meant for your offspring.

Rule of the kitchen: if you're in the kitchen, clean it up. This means no arguing about whose mess is whose, no mess, no frustration, always a clean kitchen.

Washing. I wash and hang out, they bring in, fold and put away. Pay for someone else to do your ironing. The time you spend ironing is more lucrative spent in your business.

 **119** Hire a cleaner, and any other assistance you need.

The ultimate in delegation is to hire a cleaner. Many people say, 'I can't afford it.' How much do you spend on lunches and snacks right now? A couple of hours will only cost between $30 and $45. You'll come home to a clean house, and Saturday can be spent on life-enriching pursuits instead of embracing a broom and a toilet brush! You don't have to be on a high income to manage some kind of help.

> My children were very young and my budget very stretched when my wise family doctor gave me some great advice. He also had a family of six, so he understood my challenges very well.
>
> 'Find a local schoolgirl who can come in and help you during hell hour. (A time which all parents of small children correctly interpret as somewhere between 4 and 6 p.m.!) She can peel potatoes, bring in the washing, tidy up the house, help bathe the kids, whatever you need help with.'
>
> It was a brilliant suggestion. I immediately reshuffled my pennies, found a young girl down the road willing to work for a small hourly rate, and employed her until the older children were big enough to start helping with the chores.

And what about lawn mowing, car washing, window cleaning, gardening, and sending out the ironing? If you enjoy doing all these, great. On the other hand, if you can think of better ways to spend your time, and can afford a small outgoing in return for freedom, give someone else the opportunity to make some money.

 Look for streamlined ways to help you keep the household chores under control.

There are always better ways of doing things. Keep your ear to the ground, ask your mates for their best time-saving tips, and you'll be surprised at the great ideas that pop up.

➡ Put as many of your regular payments on automatic payment as you can.

➡ File all your bills in the one place as soon as they come in, and make a diary note in your organiser to remind you to pay them on the due date.

➡ If you've got a garden, what about investing in a timed watering-system? This saves either spending a lot of time in the summer shifting hoses, or a very limp and unexciting garden in the sweltering months of the year.

This last one came from one of my training programme participants.

'My very organised sister (single parent/teacher) felt stressed about looking after her home, so she put together an annual diary to check things like the roof, plumbing, dates for insurance, all those responsibilities. Now she can relax and not feel anxious or guilty.'

Conclusion

To help me say goodbye, I'd like to share the following pearls of wisdom. I don't know if he wrote it, but the poem comes from John Grogan's tape *Secrets of Time Management Success*.

I am your constant companion. I am your greatest helper or your heaviest burden.

I will push you onward or drag you down to failure. I am at your command.

Half of the tasks that you do, you may just as well turn over to me and I will do them quickly and correctly.

I am easily managed; you must merely be firm with me.

Show me exactly how you want something done. After a few lessons, I will do it automatically.

I am the servant of all great people, and alas, of all failures as well. Those who are great, I have made great. And those who are failures, I have made failures.

I am not a machine but I work with all the precision of a machine plus the intelligence of a person.

You may run me for profit or run me for ruin, it makes no difference to me.

Take me, train me, be firm with me and I will lay the work at your feet. Be easy with me and I will destroy you.

Who am I?

Habit is my name.

Enjoy using time – your greatest gift – to the full. In doing so you will live the life of your dreams.

Index